To Caroline ~

[signature]

WINNING THE IMAGE GAME

WINNING THE IMAGE GAME

❖   ❖   ❖

A Ten Step Masterplan
for Achieving Power, Prestige, and Profit

by

Bobbie Gee

PageMill Press

BERKELEY·CALIFORNIA

Winning the Image Game
A Ten Step Masterplan for Achieving Power, Prestige and Profit

For information address
PageMill Press, 2716 Ninth Street, Berkeley, California 94710-2606

President and Publisher: Tamara C. Traeder
Editorial Director: Roy M. Carlisle
Copyeditor: Shirley Loffer
Jacket design: Paula Schlosser
Typeset by Cragmont Publications, Oakland, California
Typographic specifications: Text is 10 point ITC Stone Serif
    on 14 points lead. Chapter titles are ITC Stone Sans Bold,
    and subheads are ITC Stone Sans Semibold.
Printed in the United States of America

First Printing, May 1991
Second Printing, July 1991
Third Printing, June 1993

DEDICATION

This book is dedicated to three exceptional people who have brought great happiness and love into my life.

My husband, Ernie, who through his life examples of respect, dignity and kindness, has taught me the meaning of unconditional love.

Kellie and Tracy, my best friends and the most genuine, loving daughters a mother could have.

I love you all.

ACKNOWLEDGMENTS

The publication of this book gives me the opportunity to thank all of those who have made it possible.

My parents Stanton and Margaret Harrison for their life lessons.

My sister, Janelle Bulza for always believing in me.

To Roy M. Carlisle, my editor and the Editorial Director of PageMill Press: Had we not met, I sincerely believe this book never would have been completed. Thank you for your dedication and for being a person I could believe in.

To Bob Phelps who gave me my Disneyland job in 1975.

To Marcia Kear who was there in the beginning, and Sharon Jones who made sense out of those notes, and Sausha Sherbin, who was there when I needed her.

To Shari Bebb who asked the right questions, and to Pat Means who got me organized, and to Phil Ruggerio who contributed to the right tone in the book, my sincere thanks for all of your collaborative efforts.

Many people have been involved in making this book a reality. Some encouraged, others listened and a few, had to make sense out of my chaotic and creative thoughts. You may be unaware of the role you played, but, to me you made a difference. I am grateful.

To all of you.

A special thank you to my heavenly Father who never has given up on me.

Contents

Prologue ix

1 Playing the Image Game in the 1990s 1

2 Masterplanning Your Business Image 13

3 Your Foundation *Begin at the Beginning* 25

4 Your External Image *Elephants and Mosquitoes* 37

5 Your Internal Image *The Hidden Half* 59

6 The Emotional Connection *The Essential Ingredient* 81

7 Maintaining Your Image 99

8 Lifestyle and Likability 113

9 Image from the Inside Out 121

10 The Balancing Game 135

PROLOGUE

Many people harbor the mistaken belief that the word "image" is only used in the context of personal presentation. But it connotes much, much more. Image also refers to that ambience, aura and mystique that surround a few lucky businesses, products, and people. Experience teaches that when business leaders understand the principles of image and image-making, they reap the reward in the form of increased profits.

Over the past ten years I have circled the globe consulting and speaking on the fascinating topic of corporate image, image perception, and customer relations. My travels have taken me to sixteen different countries on five continents. I have spoken to Fortune 500 companies and small entrepreneurial businesses. Groups both large and small have honored me with invitations to keynote their conventions and conferences.

Is there really such widespread interest in imagemaking for business? Just read the news headlines from the last couple of years: "Airlines Concentrate on Corporate Image," "Meat Industry Gears Up To Give Beef a Leaner, Healthier Image," "Chief Justice Urges Lawyers to Clean Up Image," "Public Commodity Funds Acquire Bad Image That Won't Fade Soon," and "Japanese Firms Learning Art of Image Polishing."

As fate would have it, I was given an opportunity to begin my career in image training at the tender age of seventeen. It was my work with the Walt Disney Company that helped me realize just how encompassing the topic of image is, not only in the United States but around the world. Since then, my understanding of the power and meaning of image has deepened. I have spent my entire professional life collecting material and developing the philosophy and insights I offer in this book.

My desire is that readers will recognize the importance of building a positive image and apply that desire both in business and in personal life. I began writing my book several years ago, and found that not only my knowledge but the subject itself continued to grow and change. Consequently, I was constantly revising the manuscript. But what became clear is that there is no end to understanding this topic, nor to the numerous applications of that knowledge to every type of business, organization, or institution. In the two years since the first publication of this book, our fast-paced society has witnessed a sea of changes, as I anticipated. But the principles I've outlined remain true and helpful still.

The 90's are fast becoming the decade of the small-business entrepreneur. My belief is that a strategic and well-planned business and personal life is extremely important, not only for the small business entrepreneur, but for the large corporation and CEO as well. In the small business, you put yourself and your livelihood on the line every day. Your reputation is at risk every time you interface with customers. Your customers' perception of your image now becomes their truth, their reality. That initial first impression can be critical for sales and continued patronage. It is even more important because you do not have an established corporate tradition or years of identification with your product or service. The principles outlined in this book are not just a masterplan for a corporate giant—they are designed with the small business owner very much in mind.

The image of some of the companies used as illustrations in this book have shifted with time. Images need constant attention as times and the business climate change. Since this book was written, IBM has encountered a crisis in its own image that has been accompanied by a sharp downturn of its bottom line. Very recently, McDonalds has successfully weathered a challenge to its environmental sensitivity. These two very large businesses must pay attention to image as carefully as any small or medium-sized enterprise. Every aspect of your business, from its product to its employees, project an image, even though the fact may go unrecognized. Whether it is positive or negative depends on what you make of it.

I've had the privilege to speak on behalf of successful companies such as the Ritz-Carlton Hotel chain (winners of the Malcolm Baldridge Award), which has adopted a service strategy based on total quality management. At the Ritz-Carlton every employee is responsible for maintaining the company's image and striving to achieve 100% customer satisfaction. They have centered their full attention upon all the elements of their image—foundation, external, internal, and the intangible image. These facets of image and public perception are discussed in this book; taken together, they become essential elements in implementing a masterplan. Continuing to win the image game means never resting on your laurels—while you are relaxing, your competitors will pass you by!

My hope is that each reader will come to see how the ideas in this book are consistent with cutting-edge business perspectives and challenges. The successful image and public perception we build must be based on a foundation of respect for values, respect for people, quality products, and quality service.

Later in this book, I cite the two cardinal rules that govern the preservation of a successful business image:

(1) Remain true to your foundation, because it is responsible for the success you now enjoy.
(2) Never sacrifice long term image for short term profit.

Today and every day, we are all building toward the future, and for each edition of this work, these two golden rules still hold true!

I am hoping that you find this an informative and enjoyable book to read. Interesting stories and anecdotes abound in this intriguing, if frequently misunderstood, area of business life. So besides the step-by-step master plan, I have included many illustrations in order to highlight the making and breaking of image by individuals and businesses. My goal for you, after having read this book, is to apply all of the elements of image-making to your own situation. There is no doubt in my mind that you will see the power, influence, and profits that result from creating a more positive image.

The subject of image is vast and includes all aspects of business and personal life. Reading this book will help shed new light on this broad topic and most importantly help you successfully to incorporate "imagizing" into your own business and personal philosophy.

Bobbie Gee
Laguna Beach
May 1993

1

Playing the Image Game
in the 1990s

The 1980s was the decade when corporations and businesses discovered the power of reputation, the power of *image*. Simply put, image and reputation are the most important elements in determining who the winners and losers will be in business and public life.

We have seen the reputation of entire industries topple overnight as yesterday's superstars become today's pariahs. Insider trading on Wall Street, financial mismanagement in the savings and loan industry, fraud among defense contractors, and scandals among politicians and televangelists have destroyed the lifetime fortunes of companies and individuals. Their reputation and image were destroyed in a moment.

These highly publicized examples are just the tip of the iceberg. The images of numerous industries as diverse as the airline, auto, and banking industries and the professions of law, insurance, and medicine have all deteriorated seriously in the public's eye in recent years. All the losers in the image game violated the cardinal rule of corporate success: never sacrifice long-term reputation and image for the sake of short-term gain.

Years ago I received a book entitled *What They Think of Me Is None of My Business*. Contrary to that statement, what they think is vital to your success. It is the foundation of a successful, profitable business.

In theory, "I don't care what they think" sounds confident,

but in practice it is arrogant, destructive, and self-defeating. Who are *they* that are so easily dismissed? These people are the customers, employees, community, and the media. They elect you to office, buy your products, or use your services. They are the people who establish your business reputation. They are the people who perceive your image to be either positive or negative. What they think will determine your failure or success.

Government research shows that when one person has a negative experience, twenty or more people will eventually hear about it. You must make it your business to find out what people think and how they perceive you and your product or service.

A business puts its reputation on the line even in the most casual encounters. If people encounter inaccuracy, indifference, poor quality service or products, they will tell others. Likewise, when people experience excellent service, a premium quality product, and a genuine caring attitude, they will spread the word quickly.

EVERY BUSINESS HAS AN IMAGE

Take a look at the people around you. Each one of them is creating an image. Are they dressed appropriately? Do they speak well? What comes to mind when you think of these people? Do you consider them trustworthy? Can you depend on them? You have in your mind an image of each person you encounter. That image is based on what you perceive, on what you see, hear, or experience when you interact with that person.

I believe I could condense twenty-five years of experience in the area of personal and corporate imagizing with one insight on image: Everything and everybody has one!

Every product, person, business, city, and town has an image, like it or not. Image is what you think of when a person, product, or place comes to mind. What is the feeling you get when you hear Detroit mentioned . . . versus Honolulu? The difference in your feelings is based on the different images you hold.

Those images will determine where you go for vacation, or what soap you buy, or in which store you will shop.

How do some foods come to be viewed as "gourmet," such as truffles or pate, while others, like grits or hamburgers, will forever be seen as rather plebeian? How did snails become escargot and fish eggs transform into caviar? The difference is mostly image. Like beauty or quality, positive image may be hard to define, but you know it when it is there.

To many, both CEOs and the general public, image appears to be some mystical aura that surrounds select products, companies, and people while totally ignoring others. In some cases, it seems to be beyond logical explanation. For instance, a positive image is what a highly intelligent Richard M. Nixon has a very difficult time attaining since the Watergate scandal of the early 1970's and what the late John F. Kennedy, no matter what we read in the scandal sheets, always seems to be able to maintain.

Why are the makers of Rolex watches able to sell them for $10,000 when they are manufactured for perhaps one-tenth of that figure? Does a Rolex really *do* anything different than an inexpensive Timex? What is the mystique surrounding Mercedes-Benz that allows them to be sold for over $80,000, when the Japanese are proving they can produce a high quality luxury car for about half the price? There is no doubt that part of the answer, of course, is image.

Reputation and Image

Image is a symbol of standards. You can control how the public and your customers perceive your image. Their perception of your company becomes not only their reality, but your reality as well.

Image is what brings customers to the door but reputation for a quality product or service is what keeps them coming back.

To make this clear, imagine that you own a pizza parlor. You make the finest pizza for miles around; there really is no competition. This is a fact known to the entire community. This is your reputation.

However, your restaurant is a disaster area. When the health department comes by, they stay for the day to complete all the paper work. Your customers see the dirty floors and countertops. This is your image.

If you are the only pizza parlor in town, your poor image will not hurt your profitability. However, if another pizza parlor opens and not only makes great pizza, but has clean floors and counters, you are going to be in trouble.

YOUR MOST IMPORTANT ASSETS

For years, as a consultant to some of the largest corporations in America, I have sought to make the point to CEOs that a positive image and reputation are the most important assets their companies possess. Corporate image and reputation are the first and second stories of the superstructure of all businesses. Everything else a business does is built on those first two stories. A positive reputation is your long-term objective, but the construction of a positive image is absolutely essential to the establishment of a powerful, profitable long-term reputation. Image and reputation go hand in hand.

In 1975 I began an in-depth study of major American corporations. My goal was to discover why some companies were winning and others losing in the area of corporate image. I was especially fascinated with the fact that my audiences consistently ranked IBM, The Walt Disney Company, and McDonalds at the top of the list of corporations with great public images. I found all three began by effectively positioning themselves in their particular marketplaces with a defined image. All three were established by men who understood the power of setting standards.

Asked what came to mind when they thought about the IBM image, the thousands of people I surveyed did not even mention computers. The most frequent responses were the dress standards and the professional image of IBM's representatives. Is that too superficial on which to base a corporate image? Maybe so, but quite obviously the public I surveyed concluded that any company that establishes and enforces high standards in the areas of dress and visual image must make superior products.

Positive image always prepares the way for a positive reputation on the broader, more substantive issues, like product quality. What would happen to IBM's image if it told the sales force, "Don't worry about the dress code. We're so well established, it doesn't matter anymore"? I am convinced that in a very short time the public would perceive IBM's previously high standards for product quality and service to have deteriorated as well. What is so different about IBM in the area of image? They are willing to set standards of excellence, then expect employees to meet those standards.

No Detail Is Too Small

I spent three years with the Disney organization as image and appearance coordinator for Disneyland. It was a unique opportunity to identify and study the elements that have created one of the most successful and profitable corporate images in the world. I soon learned that there were four adults for every child who came in through the gate. These adults were not drawn to Disneyland because it was a children's paradise, which it is, but because of its highly effective image as a fun, happy, and clean place.

None of this happened by accident. When Walt Disney built Disneyland, he had to turn to his insurance policy to come up with enough capital. He and his brother Roy were on the verge of bankruptcy on numerous occasions. In the early days, not even one package of nails could be purchased without the personal signature of Roy Disney. No detail was too small. But right from the start, despite extremely tight finances, Walt placed a high priority on spending for image. He knew that even before Disneyland opened people would be forming a perception of his operation.

One of Walt Disney's strokes of genius regarding image and promotion was the establishment of the weekly television show, "Disneyland." The show obviously provided advertising for the park. More important, it linked the park with the new technology of television. People would perceive Disneyland on the cutting edge of technology: it would be clean, bright, and like nothing they had ever imagined. He was already creating a carefully controlled image of Disneyland in the minds of people.

Has it paid off? Even today, it is that original attention to detail in the park that produces a flood of correspondence from around the world. Among other things, people rave about the cleanliness: "How can 64,000 people tromp through your park every day and I didn't even step on a piece of gum?"

McDonalds is another company that has defined its image goals clearly, has given attention to detail, and enforces the highest visual image standards. In addition, McDonalds has won a place in the hearts of their communities through their civic involvements, such as the Ronald McDonald Houses which aid families of seriously ill children. I will explain more about this when we examine the specifics of building a positive corporate image.

MARKETS AND IMAGE

Does a product or service have to be expensive in order to benefit from a powerful image? No. Perrier had it with water. Grey Poupon has it with mustard. Haagen-Dazs has it with ice cream. Even cat food has an effective image with Fancy Feast!

The goal of an effective image program does not have to be the creation of an elitist image. It is all a matter of effectively positioning yourself and/or your product for your target market, whatever that market might be. I mentioned that a Timex watch does not do anything substantially different from a Rolex. That is true. But, if you remember the advertising some years ago proclaiming that a Timex watch could "take a licking and keep on ticking," you can see that it was targeted for the working masses. Contrast the Timex image with that of Rolex watches, which are always displayed in the presence of gems, gold, and money. Both advertising themes are consistent with their relative target markets.

Madison Avenue insiders talk about marketing a product to the masses or the classes. I do not particularly like the smug superiority behind those labels, but they do communicate the point I am trying to make. You can use the principles of effective imagizing to position your products for a strictly middle income market (Timex) or for an upper income market (Rolex). The elements in the image plan are the same in both cases, but the images created will be enormously different.

Look at the radical difference in the images of two of America's most successful retailers: Tiffany and Wal-Mart. Both have used effective imagizing to position themselves in two very different markets.

Tiffany has been one of the preferred jewelers of the wealthy since Martin Van Buren was president of the United States. Abraham Lincoln gave his wife a Tiffany seed pearl necklace in 1861. Richard Burton gave Elizabeth Taylor a gold Tiffany dolphin clip after he made the 1964 movie *The Night of the Iguana*. Keep in mind, Tiffany does not extend discounts to anyone, regardless of fame or fortune.

Store executives still like to tell the story about President Eisenhower's visit to Tiffany to buy his wife Mamie a present. As the story is told, the conversation went something like this:

"Does the President of the United States get a discount?" asked Ike.

"Well, Abraham Lincoln didn't," the Tiffany chairman replied.

Tiffany is refinement. The successful image of catering to the wealthy is the result of a deliberate and consistent image plan, from the pricing of its exclusive perfume at $200 an ounce to its extravagant window displays.

The Tiffany image of glamor and exclusivity has been so successful that people literally beg to buy the famous blue Tiffany gift box empty, just the box. Of course, they are not for sale. Tiffany knows the key to its ongoing success is maintaining its mystique of exclusivity, and it has done it very well for over 150 years, until just recently.

Image can be a very seductive reason for buying a business as well. Avon, during a period of expansion, bought Tiffany. What happened to the Tiffany image? When the news was released that Avon, the large manufacturer and distributor of cosmetics for the home-sale market, bought Tiffany, the image Tiffany had zealously guarded was eroded. The lesson for you? You cannot buy image. Image is something you have to create.

Now think about Wal-Mart, the number-one retailer in the U.S., followed by K-Mart and Sears. Founder Sam Walton is pure Ozark, just like his Bentonville, Arkansas headquarters. He wears a Wal-Mart ball cap and drives a ten-year-old Ford pickup truck with Leroy and Kate, his two bird dogs, in the back. You would never know this soft-spoken man is one of the wealthiest men in America and a modern-day marketing genius. Even more re- markable, the principles he followed to make Wal-Mart such a success are the same that propelled Tiffany to its stature as a jeweler. He defined his market: small, rural towns with popula- tions less than 50,000. Then he created an image that was effec- tive for that market.

You will not find the rich and famous shopping at Wal-Mart for their jewelry or clothing. The company slogan at Wal-Mart is "Everyday Low Prices." The battle to be the best is over whether children's corduroy pants should be sold for $2.50 or $3.00 in order to be competitive with K-Mart. Instead of being discreetly assisted by an elegantly dressed salesperson, you will be glad- handed by a retiree the minute you step through the door of a Wal-Mart. This person's job, officially described as "people greeter," is to welcome customers as they enter the store.

But Sam Walton's company has just as powerful and success- ful an image as Tiffany, as shown in its bottom line. The thirteen hundred Wal-Mart stores sell over $20 billion of goods each year. Retail industry analysts predicted that it would be the number-one retailer in the country and it has become so.

How do you begin to create a profitable, positive image? First, target your market; know to whom you want to sell. The makers of Fancy Feast know that cats do not buy cat food, people do. After intensive market research, the makers of Fancy Feast decided to target an upscale market. Their advertising ties the elements of fine dining and gourmet eating to their cat food. Has it worked? You bet it has!

Any company can benefit from an effective image plan that is designed with its unique target audience in mind and consistently implemented throughout its entire operation. The principles work just as powerfully for discount marketers to middle America as they do for expensive products for the wealthy.

You may be thinking, "My company's not big enough to worry about image. I'm not a Tiffany or Wal-Mart. I'll wait until we grow before I begin to concern myself with imaging." I have heard that before. There is only one problem with that outlook: image is even more important for small companies and individuals launching a new business. First impressions apply to companies as well as individuals. The image, the tone that is set in the early days of a new venture, will largely determine the long-term reputation that develops.

Not too long ago I met a person on a casual basis for the first time. I had heard very little about him and, until this meeting, had not formed any image of him in my mind. As soon as we met, he had a small word of praise for me. Do you think that this went a long way in beginning to create a positive image for this person? Of course it did. In subsequent meetings this image was reinforced.

Take a lesson from the makers of Fancy Feast cat food. Anybody or any company can make a cat food. There are literally dozens of cat food brands all competing for the cat owner's dollar. What Fancy Feast did was to carve out an image niche for itself. It created the gourmet of cat foods. Is it really any different than the other cat foods? I do not know. The important idea to remember is that by portraying the right image, the product is perceived as being different, and better than the competition.

You can not afford to wait before beginning to work on imaging. You are creating an image, a perception of yourselves and your business with your customers, all the time. There is no such thing as sitting on the sidelines in the image game.

Just as there are some companies who are clear winners in the image game, others are clear losers. The same surveys I referred to earlier have consistently given the "Worst Image Award" to the U. S. Post Office. For decades the Postal Service felt so secure in its monopoly in mail delivery that it did not think it had to concern itself with customer perception or image development. As a result, its image deteriorated. Now alternate mail delivery services like Federal Express, UPS, and Airborne Express are making large inroads in the mail delivery business.

The same was true for the state of California a few years ago. A group of state officials decided to drastically cut the tourism promotion budget in order to save taxes. They were confident that the state could get along on its raw geographical charisma. Why should any state that has Disneyland, the Golden Gate Bridge, and the Pacific Ocean have to spend money on its image? The next year, California lost $766 million in tourism revenue even before the Great Earthquake of October 17, 1989.

No matter how impeccable you think your image is, you have to promote it. Never take image for granted.

Even if you find yourself in a company or an industry with a poor or slipping image, you are not beyond hope. That is the beauty of image power. There are clearly identifiable rules to the image game. Those who break them eventually lose. Those who follow the rules can turn around even the worst image.

Take New York City, for example. Ten years ago when I mentioned New York as my next business trip or convention stop, I invariable heard comments about carrying Mace or warnings to watch out for muggers. New York had a terrible image problem. But the city tackled the problem head on and launched the highly successful, and often copied, "I love N. Y." campaign. This program helped to revitalize its tourism, but one program does not an image make.

Japan is another fabulous example. "Made in Japan" certainly does not project the same image today as it did thirty years ago. Japanese automobiles are not the most expensive cars on the market, but they have developed great prestige with the American people.

What about the radical shift in Russia's image under the leadership of Mikhail Gorbachev? No matter what your political perspective, it is undeniable that one man has, in a very short period of time, significantly changed the way the western world views the Soviet Union. He created this change partially through the skillful use of the principles of positive image-making.

My favorite example of a transformed image is the Chrysler Corporation under the leadership of Lee Iacocca. Ten years ago, the company teetered on the edge of bankruptcy, with a miniscule market share and a reputation as the maker of the car of choice of the geriatric set. I will never forget the experience I had while speaking at a convention in 1979. I was giving a presentation on the principles of sound image-making and was drawing out audience reaction to the image of various products and companies.

"Does anyone in this auditorium happen to own a Chrysler?" I asked. Nobody moved. Nobody made a sound. You could have heard a pin drop. I knew, based on the laws of statistical probability, there had to be at least forty or fifty Chrysler owners in an audience of that size.

"Surely, someone here owns a Chrysler," I persisted. Nothing. Then I spotted her. An older lady near the front, obviously fidgeting and avoiding my eyes. I walked over to the spot on the platform nearest to this dear lady, locked my gaze on her, and with my sweetest smile repeated, "Surely, s-o-m-e-one here owns a Chrysler?" That did it. Rolling her eyes in resignation and nodding her head, the woman stood to her feet and said, "Yes, Honey, I do. And, if you think that's bad . . . I own a Chrysler dealership". The audience roared!

Iacocca and the Chrysler team changed all that. Young Americans are no longer ashamed to admit they own a Chrysler.

However, without constant monitoring, image and reputation change, sometimes for the worse.

Beyond Advertising

There is an old saying that you can't turn a sow's ear into a silk purse. The truth of that saying becomes readily apparent when companies depend only on advertising to project their image to the American consumer. Advertising is necessary to the image master plan. In fact, eighty-one of the one hundred largest U. S. corporations are currently spending $500 million a year just to advertise their corporations. This is above and beyond what they are spending to promote their products. They know the importance of their company's image to bottom-line profits.

However, the construction of a positive long-term image involves more than spending money on an advertising campaign. The history of consumer America is littered with the bones of products from the Edsel to the "new Coke" that have failed to capture the public's approval despite incredibly large advertising budgets. Advertising alone will not create a positive, powerful image, regardless of how much money is spent.

2

Masterplanning Your Business Image

Everyone wants a powerful, profitable business image. But only a handful in every industry, in every city, make it into the winner's circle. The benefits of being part of that elite group are enormous. A sterling reputation, prestige, and financial success are just some of the rewards of winning the corporate image game.

While there are many companies and people losing the image game, the 1980s produced some pronounced winners. Companies such as Wal-Mart, PepsiCo and Boeing, as well as scores of others, have been quietly winning the image war for the hearts and minds (and pockets) of the American public. They are winning while others are losing because they understand the importance of image and the need for a comprehensive, multifaceted image plan.

If the rewards are so great, why do so few win? Because it is not easy. It is easy to throw money at an advertising agency and hope it can win the image war for you. What is hard is to establish standards of excellence, develop a comprehensive image plan, and work that plan over a period of time.

If you believe that a positive, attention-getting, money-making image will evolve on its own with a quality product, quality service, and good intentions, you are probably wrong. If by chance it does happen on its own, it could take years. With a strategic image plan, those years could, and would, be cut in half.

WHY CREATE A MASTERPLAN?

But you may still be asking why is the Image Masterplan really necessary? Many businesses have one or two image areas developed—perhaps an effective name and logo or an adequate advertising thrust. Some have four or five. But in my experience, having only a handful of the image elements in operation can be worse than having none at all. A company without a comprehensive plan represents itself inconsistently to the public. That is, the public hears one thing from the company, hears one set of claims, and sees something else. The result can be a serious credibility gap.

Let us say, for instance, that your airline has just invested huge amounts in an advertising campaign centered around the slogan "We are your friends in the sky." The advertising campaign was launched. But the employees were never trained in how to carry out the philosophy. So there was a gap between advertising claims and the experience of customers on the front lines. Your customers might eventually conclude that you are not their friends after all.

The result of an incomplete image plan is image backlash. It is the kind of thing CEOs have nightmares about. When image backlash occurs, the public's perception of the company is even lower than it would have been if the company had no advertising campaign at all. It may take years to undo the damage. But it does not have to be that way. What is needed is to extend the imagizing process a bit to include not just two or three, but all areas of the Image Masterplan.

One of my clients is a major financial institution. It had a carefully developed company campaign centered on being "The Bank of the Future." After a thorough image analysis I pointed out that many of their branch offices displayed a 1950s color scheme and decor. The customers were walking into the bank hearing one thing "The Bank of the Future" and seeing another the 1950s. The public's very understandable reaction is that this is just one more example of false corporate sloganeering. The company becomes less believable, and its image and reputation are actually diminished, rather than enhanced, by its advertising. All that was needed was to extend the imagizing process into the visual area to create a unified image.

Another reason for an Image Masterplan is that it can carry you through times of trouble, for example, through a recession. When money is in short supply, your customers will think twice before making a purchase. They will turn to the businesses with the best reputation and image for standing behind their products.

Manufacturers must keep a stable of attorneys ready at all times to defend not only the quality of their product, but their long-term reputation as well. Anyone spending a few hours watching television will see advertisements by attorneys encouraging lawsuits. A focused Image Masterplan might save you from a devastating judgment. At the current rate of lawsuits and the vision of easy money, masterplanning your image may be essential to survival in business. When you go to court, you definitely need image on your side.

The companies with Image Masterplans are some of the most successful in the country. That is why masterplanning a business image is probably the single most important step a company can take to position itself ahead of its competition. If it sounds too tough, remember that it is even harder to succeed in the long run in today's competitive business world without an image plan.

THE BUILDING BLOCKS OF THE MASTERPLAN

The Image Masterplan has four main parts: *the foundation, the external image, the internal image, and the intangible image.* Each part of the plan is geared to achieve three significant objectives:

(1) To be more competent and effective with your customers,

(2) To maintain that all-important image of success that gives your customers confidence in you, and,

(3) To establish an emotional connection with the customer
and the public.

The Image Masterplan will create a solid foundation for effective internal and external images. A company's external image is the way that company is perceived externally by the public, the media, and its investors. Its internal image is the way the company is perceived internally by its employees and management.

The internal image of a company ultimately affects the way it is viewed by the public. The internal, employee-related aspects of a business image are often overlooked in image programs. Traditional image programs focus almost exclusively on the external and visual aspects of image. My research has shown that the intangible areas of employee attitude and morale have as significant an effect on the long-term reputation of a business as do the more tangible and visible elements in the image package. Your employees represent your company to the public. Your employees make the all-important emotional connection with your customer.

Although hard to define, the charismatic atmosphere that surrounds many positive image companies, and the imagizing process, does not have to be mysterious. I have identified the key elements in any effective, comprehensive image plan.

> Establishing a Foundation
> External Imaging
> > Product Quality
> > Tangible Image—The Five Senses
> > Advertising
> > Community Involvement
> > Media Relations
> > Investor Relations
> > Employee Attitude & Appearance
> Internal Imaging
> > Financial Plan
> > Employment Policies

Employee Orientation and Training
Employee Recognition Program
Intangible Image
Ego of Customer
Self-Image of Customer

Some of the elements are more obvious, such as the tangible image of the company or product: the name, logo, and signage. Equally important are a host of other factors, often overlooked or neglected, the development of a written company philosophy, for instance. The company philosophy and the image slogan that is derived from it are the foundation of the image plan.

The other critical, but often neglected, elements in the image plan revolve around the internal image of the company, that is, the actions and attitudes of the employees. The fostering of employee morale is crucial to this part of the image plan. Everything from employee advancement opportunities to recognition programs comes into play in creating this internal aspect of the business image.

Before I go any further, I need to define some terms for you. By taking a few moments now, your understanding of imagizing will be facilitated.

Tangible: What customers see, smell, hear, touch, and taste. (*first impressions*)

Intangible: Customers' responses to the tangible plus their reactions to the actions and attitudes of the company employees. (*how the customer feels*)

Internal: The atmosphere within the organization; the positive or negative interactions of employees with management, policies, and procedures. (*employee loyalty*)

External: The impact of the three previous areas, plus the general public's opinion of the company as influenced by its advertising, product quality, media relations, and community service. (*public perceptions*)

As I have already said, a positive image involves a lot more than a good advertising campaign. It is a complex, multifaceted, synergistic plan. Each part is affected by the other parts. The plan is most effective when all the parts work together. Before we discuss the key elements of a comprehensive image plan in detail it will be helpful to quickly summarize each of the four major areas of the plan—the foundation, external image, internal image, and intangible image. In this way you can evaluate your own situation within the framework of the whole Masterplan.

Foundation

Your foundation supports the development and maintenance of a consistent, powerful, and positive image. There are five steps to creating your image and reputation foundation.

A solid foundation begins with a thorough review of your business principles. Based on the commitment to your principles you can now develop your mission statement. Then it is time to condense this set of principles into a simple short working corporate philosophy. The next step is to identify your specific long-term goals. A clear sense of direction is essential in developing your image Masterplan.

After you know what you want to achieve then you must decide what standards your employees will follow in helping you achieve your goals.

The disciplines or standards that must be set up in order to support your long term goals can now be written more easily. They will follow out of this process of review, goal setting, and identification. Maintaining your standards or disciplines will become the method by which your foundation will remain intact.

External Image

The external image program has six elements.

Product quality is the first element and most important to your long-term business reputation. Advertising may bring customers in, but customer satisfaction over time depends on the quality of your product or service. No amount of well-financed imagizing can make up for a shoddy product.

Tangible image is the way your business is perceived by the five senses—what the public sees, hears, feels, smells, and touches. This element covers everything from company name and logo to office decor and letterhead.

For larger companies, advertising is the introduction of your products and services to the public. Some advertising builds a powerful image; some obviously does not. How clearly does your advertising communicate your uniqueness? How well does it spell out the ways in which you are different from your competitors? Does the advertising connect emotionally with the viewers? Have you clearly defined your market, so that you can position your advertising image to reach that market? There are a number of issues, other than budget, that determine whether advertising is effective.

Most of us would rather do business with people we perceive to be givers. Thus, community involvement is an important part of a company's external image program. Charitable giving not only benefits the local community; it also is another way of fostering an emotional connection with the public.

Whether a company is big or small, media relations is an increasingly significant part of any image program. The free publicity the media provides may be good or bad depending on whether you have invested time in cultivating contacts in the media or prepared press releases and other publicity material that make a journalist's or editor's job easier.

And finally, for many CEOs in today's venture capital world, investor relations is an absolutely essential part of the corporate image program. If the proper foundation has been laid in the other image areas, the task of extending the image program to include investors is significantly easier. Unfortunately, many CEOs find themselves without an effective image program in place with the public; then throw together a hastily designed public relations package for investors. No special "dog and pony show" for investors can make up for a poor image with the public.

Common sense should prevail in the sixth area of external image. Employee appearance and personality are more important than most companies realize. It is a critical component of the first impression a customer might have of your company. But common sense 101 is seldom taught in our institutions of higher learning. Therefore appearance and personality problems remain an annoyance. Yet as annoying as they are employee appearance and personality are vital to winning the image game.

Internal Image

Now let us turn our attention inside the company. Often it would seem a priority to develop a financial plan before developing a masterplan. It is, of course, very important to develop a financial plan very early in the game but it should come after the masterplan has been developed. In addition to the practical budgeting process for operations there must be an intelligent understanding of how to budget for image. This may include using visualization techniques in order to accurately assess what people will say about your company, and how they will experience your products or services. This process will also help you maximize your image potential in the specific niche of the market that you are targeting your products or services for with regard to customers and vendors.

Internal image programs foster employee loyalty and morale. The three programs affecting internal image are employment policies, employee orientation and training, and employee recognition programs.

Employment policies include a number of basic areas that affect employee morale: salary, position authority, opportunity for advancement, perks, and internal communication.

Employee orientation and training is the key to employees understanding the vision and standards of the company. Training provides the instruction and motivation employees need to represent the company effectively to customers. Employee training and orientation determine employees' effectiveness in connecting emotionally to the company first and then with customers, serving them competently and professionally.

Finally, employee recognition programs are one of the most powerful yet most cost-effective ways of building high employee morale and motivation. They touch that most basic of human emotional needs, the need to feel important and appreciated.

Business image has to do with how the public perceives your company. You can improve that perception by the way you train your employees internally to serve your customers and if your training maintains standards of excellence.

Intangible Image

Nice, kind, understanding, sympathetic. Frustration, irritation, anger, rejection. All of these words describe feelings. Feelings may not reflect reality but nonetheless they affect our judgments. Those judgments affect our buying decisions. So intangible image is all about feelings. Therefore intangible image is about your success at connecting to the ego and emotional dimensions of your customers and the public.

This is all hard work and no amount of discussion or understanding changes that reality. It involves working the multifaceted plan described in the next three chapters. But the long-term rewards are nothing less than a solid reputation, prestige, a healthy bottom line—fulfilling the purposes of positive image projection.

Monitoring the Traffic Flow

Every company today wants a positive image. By knowing and understanding how elements of an image plan work together, you can lead your company to a powerful positive image or create a new image. However, very few are willing to do the work necessary to construct an image and to establish the foundation for that all-important long-term reputation. A company may do well in several of the key image plan areas, perhaps even a majority of them. But if any aspects are allowed to slide too far too long, the overall image and reputation of the company will be seriously affected.

You may say, "I leave all of that image stuff up to my public relations company." Hiring a public relations firm is fine, but give them something with which to work. Do you realize how many thousands of dollars you could save yourself if you first had an image plan, if you first start to practice the principles I give you in this book? Do you realize how much more control you would have if you went to them with a positive image already in place and working? Put my principles to work, first, then hire a public relations firm.

Any business can benefit from an effective image plan designed with its unique target market in mind. The principles of imagizing work just as powerfully for discount products as they do for expensive items, but the work must be focused. Some companies, like Sears and J. C. Penney, seem to be unsure of what their image is or how to make it work.

A number of years ago I called Penney's corporate offices and asked to speak to the person responsible for the company's image overhaul. I was put on hold for awhile then transferred to the public relations department. I explained that I was writing a book on business image and wanted to talk with them about their new image strategy. I was quickly disposed of in a rude and abrupt manner. It seems that Penney's had the right idea, but no one person coordinating the masterplan who could discuss their strategy with me. Isn't and shouldn't phone etiquette be a part of fulfilling a positive image?

What is Penney's doing? They were trying to upgrade the image by "importing" designer labels and implementing an extensive remodeling program. Is substantial training for its employees provided to compliment the new image it wants to project? Are they re-evaluating their employee standards? Not that I could tell.

Is Penney's accomplishing what it set out to do? Will they be able to change their image with the public? Image is a two-way street that must be carefully monitored. The traffic moves in two directions: from the corporate office to the consumer and back. If there is not an equal amount of traffic in each direction, no matter how well planned, any new image plan is doomed to fail.

Decor and designer labels alone will not make a new image. It takes dedication at all levels to create a new, strong corporate identity. You cannot cash in on someone else's image. It must be your own. It begins with a solid, carefully planned foundation. Will Penney's win the image game? They are in the process of upgrading the appearance of their stores and it is obvious that people do perceive that they are updating their image. I do sincerely hope they will win the image game because they are a solid part of America's retail history.

Sears is another corporate giant who is struggling with the direction of their image. It would be interesting to sit in on one of their board meetings. I wonder who they perceive as their competition, where they fit in the image game? The Wall Street Journal has repeatedly reported earnings losses over the last few years for this giant chain. In contrast another large chain with a different image strategy, Wal-Mart, has maintained a clear sense of where they fit in the market, who their customers really are, and how to keep their image clean and positive. Who would have thought that a company like Sears could go through such confusing years over their image identity.

3

Your Foundation
Begin at the Beginning

The first step in the implementation of your Image Masterplan, is to establish a foundation. A set of values, goals, principles and philosophies upon which the over-all plan will rest. Your Image Masterplan will never achieve the powerful results you want unless the plan is supported by unbending steel, set in bedrock. Without the five foundation elements, all else is superficial. Take time, do not rush the preparation and construction of your Image foundation.

Executives who are too busy running their businesses to take the needed time to develop a proper foundation and Image Masterplan are like people who are too busy working to take the time to develop a long-term financial plan for their retirement. Eventually, it all catches up with you.

Before a building is erected, a foundation must be constructed. The taller the building, the deeper the foundation. The importance of a good foundation was graphically explained to me when I was in San Francisco just after the '89 earthquake. In riding around the town, I noticed some buildings of only two or three stories were completely demolished. However, buildings of twenty, thirty, and even forty stories survived the quake with little more than superficial damage. I asked an engineer how that could be possible. The engineer gave me a one-sentence explanation: "Because the foundations were designed and built to withstand the stresses of a trauma, and the buildings were bolted to their foundations."

I was fascinated by the correlation. For a building to successfully survive a major earth shaking trauma, it must be bolted to a proper foundation. And, for a business, corporation, country, or even a family to survive, they must, also, be bolted down to a proper foundation. It sounds too ridiculous to even imagine a building contractor disregarding the foundation as unnecessary, after all, who will see it. Yet time and time again, I interface with organizations that have neglected this very issue.

What does being bolted to a strong foundation mean when it comes to building a successful business? It means that even though things get a bit rocky—there are reversals in business, or you receive negative press—you will have an increased chance of survival.

What goes into building an effective foundation for a successful business? Just as there are specific regulations for the foundation of a building, there are specific ingredients for the foundation of a successful business. These elements are:

1. Principles
2. Mission Statement
3. Philosophy
4. Long-term goals
5. Standards

Ignoring these five essential ingredients could mean disaster. If you want to build a successful business that has a positive image, you will study the five items that belong in your foundation, develop, use and stay true to them.

STEP 1. YOUR MORAL PRINCIPLES

Your principles are the cornerstone of your foundation. For some, this is the most overlooked area when developing a business plan. More than at any time in our history, major business failures can be traced to unethical or moral mistakes in judgement.

Know what you believe and what you believe in. Know what you stand for. To make the process of identifying your principles a little easier, first, write down the one commitment in your life you would not, under any circumstances, change. Now, clearly state your definition of a principled person.

It is a wise person who identifies their principles and it is an intelligent company who does the same. When your principles are clearly defined there is a feeling of completeness. Life will change but principles do not change.

One evening upon closing a small grocery store in Rule, Texas, the seventeen year old clerk realized that he had mistakenly overcharged his final customer of the day by ten cents. Knowing his customer had fallen on hard times his conscience got the best of him. This teenager set out on foot, walked two miles and returned the dime. If you find this story impossible to believe it is because we live in the 1990's and the story took place in 1870. The man was my great grandfather. He became well known for his honesty and acts of kindness. This story has been repeated many times, leaving its positive affect on each generation. I apologize for going back 130 years, but the past 40 years have been tough times for principles. These days I often get requests to speak on the topic of returning to the basics. The pendulum has been slow to return, but it will. Maybe not in my lifetime, but it will. Principles are eternal.

For some, this is the most overlooked area when developing a business plan. As you begin to develop your principles of doing business, you will find they are interwoven with your personal principles—one will influence the other.

Why are business principles so important? Webster's dictionary defines principle as "[a] fixed or predetermined policy or mode of action." The establishment of principles, written principles, will guide you and your employees to what actions to take when facing day-to-day problems or a crisis.

You might ask, "What do principles have to do with making money, with the success of my business?" Let us say you own a car dealership. You want to sell 2,000 cars this year and you tell this to your sales force. There are two basic ways to explain this goal: you can say, "Do whatever it takes" or you can say, "We're going to sell these cars so that we will get referrals and return business. We will treat the customer with respect." The principle expressed in the first statement leaves the method of sales open to abuse, perhaps even dishonesty. The second statement reflects principles that are honest and aboveboard. If you are planning to be in business for the long haul, it benefits you to express the principles of the second statement in writing for all to read.

Kenneth C. Nichols, past chairman, American Council of Life Insurance, wrote in the December 4, 1989 issue of Financial Services Week the following:

"The life insurance industry's poor public image is largely of its own making. Little will change until industry offices take a cold, hard look at themselves and many of the industry's questionable practices. There has been a lot of talk around about getting back to the basics in business and I think we need to get back to something very basic; the integrity of conduct—how we conduct our business and serve our customers."

Continue by clearly stating your definition of a principled company. To possess a great reputation means to be principle-centered. Whether you are the ship's rudder for 3000 employees or one ten year old child, let principles be your guiding light. All remaining blocks of your foundation will now lean on your cornerstone.

STEP 2. MISSION STATEMENT

A mission statement is a commission. It means sending forth to perform a stipulated service. A definite task or errand. A mission statement is a charge. Your mission statement is your internal driving force. Your mission statement works as a beacon giving direction, insight, and vision to all involved.

1. Be specific. I recently attended the year end managers meeting of a fast growing Southern California company. Even though the company had been in business many years, no formal mission statement existed. The meeting began with the reading of the newly written mission statement. As best I can recall, the gist went something like this, "The best possible service at the lowest possible price." The idea is of value, of course, but, the message was far too general in scope. A hundred thousand companies could have adopted the same statement. Be specific. Your mission statement should give direction with a goal—an end result.

I wonder. Did the Japanese say, "Our mission is to build a better car for the American market", or, did they say, "Our mission is to build cars so superior to those presently being manufactured by General Motors, Ford and Chrysler, that the American consumers will buy 3 million cars a year from us. We will build these cars to be cost efficient and cost effective. We will reward the customer with superb service and gratitude."

2. Make it inspiring. Your statement must inspire your employees. It should reflect your business ideals and the standards of excellence to which you are committed. As you consider your company vision and purpose, "GO for the best." Nothing less will inspire others.

3. Make it honest and accurate. Do not include anything you are not prepared to deliver. If you make a statement regarding customer service hoping to inspire your employees, but, the organization's leaders are clearly only interested in profit and loss, your mission statement will, at once, be a counterfeit.

4. Share your long term vision. Sharing your long term vision gives your employees insight into your corporate goals. How can I, as an employee, help you arrive at your destination when I don't know where we are going?

5. Focus on human needs. The most successful mission statements have a clear and unswerving commitment to meeting some human need through products and services. Those companies that are in business only for the purpose to make money, or, to become the biggest in their industry, eventually suffer from serious image deterioration. Your company mission statement should clearly identify the felt needs of the customer that you are committed to meeting.

STEP 3. YOUR PERSONAL AND BUSINESS PHILOSOPHY

The third block used to form your foundation is a statement of philosophy. Using the first two elements of your foundation; principles and your mission statement, develop a corporate philosophy. Your corporate philosophy is different than the above as it will be stated in as few words as possible.

As an example, "Cleanliness, quality and service," is one of the best and most famous corporate philosophies in the corporate world today. When I consult with a company, I ask the CEO to write the first draft of the company's mission statement. The result is often a full page which is, then, condensed into a couple of paragraphs. Those two paragraphs are then condensed to the fewest number of words necessary to make our point and that becomes your corporate philosophy. This process is absolutely crucial to the development of a focused, unified image package. It is worth doing right. Do not confuse an advertising slogan and a corporate philosophy.

Once again, generalizations like, "We care," or "Putting the customer first," seldom inspire excellence. Your employees want and need to know what makes you different. As an example, "A tradition of progress," might be a good ad slogan, but, is not a philosophy. Compare that to Disney's, "We create happiness." This tells the employee exactly what their job is in terms of the corporate image. Get out there and make people happy.

A few years ago, I was a consultant to the Ice Capades Chalet Division of Metro Media Corporation. In our initial session, I said to the president, "You've been in business forty years. What is your corporate philosophy?" He thought for a minute then looked up and said, "You know, I don't think we have one."

Unfortunately, this is more the rule than the exception. Most companies operate without a clearly defined corporate philosophy. A statement of philosophy is absolutely essential to a clear understanding of what the company stands for and expects to achieve.

If you develop a corporate philosophy such as, "We build only the best," you must be prepared to buy only the finest parts and materials, or your image will disintegrate from the inside out. "We build only the best," is not only a great employee motivator, it is, also, a great ad slogan.

During my consulting with Ice Capades, we discovered that one of the problem areas was the company's skating classes. The teachers were trying to turn every child into a skilled, technical skater. As we thought through the corporate philosophy, we eventually came up with the image slogan, "We create fun!" That simple slogan became the North Star for restructuring the atmosphere of the skating rinks. Employees were trained to help children have fun during classes. Sagging profits began to climb.

Nordstrom Retail Stores has taken, "The only difference between us and the store down the street is, the way we treat our customers," to new heights of customer service. To develop a successful image, you need to be different and to promote that difference.

In writing your overall philosophy, try to identify what makes you different from your competitors. List as many of these key differences as you can identify. This will allow you to develop an image that will position you as absolutely unique in you field.

During this time of introspection, it is also wise to write your personal philosophy. After one year of thought and many questions, I decided on, "I will do my best to lead a guilt free life." This philosophy was the end result of my talks with learned medical professionals. After asking the question, "Why are there so many people who are sick and what is the main cause for so much illness?" The answer I received was that up to 90% of the people in hospitals were not ill due to an accident. They were there because their insides were eating them up.

I then asked what the main cause of this condition was. As you might expect, I was expecting to hear about poor diet or lack exercise. Instead, I heard the word, EMOTIONS. Negative emotions are eating up and destroying more people than all the french fries fast food restaurants can produce.

I then asked what emotion was doing most of the damage, and I heard the word, "Guilt." It seems, "Why did I—Why didn't I—I should have—I shouldn't have—If I only had, and so forth is a major killer and claims many people before their time. Thinking through your personal philosophy will cause you to consider your lifestyle.

The first three steps then in masterplanning your business image is to consider your principles of doing business, to write a mission statement and the development of a philosophy.

STEP 4. YOUR LONG TERM GOALS

You have to know where you are going . If you do not, how are you going to know when you have arrived? You must have long-term goals. Your goals are your road map.

There is an often used example regarding the value of long-term goals that bears repeating here. You want to drive to New York from Los Angeles by the most direct means possible. You get out maps and establish your route. A place is selected as a stop each night. Your long-term goal is New York. The short-term goals are the nightly stops. You have direction and you know where you are going; you are feeling great about the trip. This is how long-term goals affect your business.

In business, you must know your destination, what you want to achieve. By knowing your final goal, you will find that many smaller decisions have been made for you. Let us say you are in the middle of Kansas enroute to New York. Do you suddenly decide you want to see Oregon? If you are committed to reaching New York, seeing Oregon will have to wait because it is not in line with your goal.

New products and services your business may entertain must be examined in light of the question, "How will this move me closer to my goal?" If not, you run the risk of moving away from your goal and creating confusion within your organization. By establishing long-term goals, you will infuse a sense of direction and more quickly reach your goals.

STEP 5. YOUR STANDARDS FOR CONDUCT AND APPEARANCES

The final step in building a strong foundation is the establishment of written standards. Standards define the actions that support your philosophy, goals, and principles. Standards are your employees tools for maintaining and communicating your image.

When developing your standards, consider every area that could in anyway affect your image. Remember common sense is the exception. A number of years ago, after speaking for the sales rally of a large real estate franchise the divisional director invited me to dinner along with eight members of the regional office. We came directly from the meeting, therefore, all the people were wearing very recognizable career apparel.

Having come form a motivational sales rally, spirits were high and drinks were ordered. As more drinks arrived, the language, jokes and noise level, all surpassed professionalism. I watched in stunned disbelief as patrons of the restaurant became increasingly annoyed. The image of this successful company was tarnishing by the minute.

When developing standards and guidelines, cover every aspect that could in any way affect your image. Employees off duty hours are not their own, **if** they are wearing company career apparel, name or logo recognition. A true professional is recognized by his/her actions when away from the work place and when he or she thinks no one is looking. Your standards book should cover everything from appearance to specific modes of conduct to honesty to company taboos. To simply say we expect high standards is leaving the word, "high," up to personal interpretation.

One day I received a call from an office of the A. L. Williams Corporation. The person calling identified himself as the manager and stated that he wished to employ me as speaker. As we talked, I surmised that he was really interested in retaining the services of a trainer three times a week. I told him it was not realistic to consider me for such a position because I would charge the same amount as I would for a keynote address. He was insistent and arranged an appointment to talk with me at my office.

At the appointed time, two men arrived at my office—not one as had been previously arranged. It took only a few minutes for me to realize that they were attempting to recruit me to sell insurance. They did not want a speaker or trainer as was represented the day before: they wanted a new recruit. At first, I politely declined. As they became more overbearing, I became more insistent that they leave. Finally they did, but not before they had made me very angry.

Why would these two men misrepresent themselves and the company for which they worked? Is there something they felt they should hide? As I thought more about my encounter with these two men, I came to the conclusion that the A. L. Williams Corporation had not established standards of conduct for their representatives or had failed in communicating them clearly.

Employees at every level need to know what is expected of them. How will they know this? By the establishment of written standards that are a part of an employee handbook. If you spell out exactly what you expect from your employees, you will have fewer misunderstandings and problems. Do not mistake a policy and procedural manual for a standards book.

Corporate standards need to be defined. These standards should include even the smallest details. It will help to develop an overall picture of the standards needed and desired in each area of your business: from the weeds in your parking lot to the conduct of your senior executives.

Some standards will be expectations. Others will take the form of rules and still others come under the category of disciplines. The main thing is to have standards and share them with all employees. A company succeeds or fails, only through its employees. That is the best reason for taking the time to define standards.

Once you have established the foundation of your Image Masterplan, you will be ready to embark on its superstructure, your external image.

4

Your External Image
Elephants and Mosquitoes

"Elephants don't bite," goes the saying, "mosquitoes do." It is not the big things that ruin us. It is the little ones. That is definitely true of image. It is all the little things we fail to give attention to that rob us of success.

It has been said that Walt Disney's fanatical attention to detail in Disneyland arose out of a disastrous visit he and his children paid to B-grade amusement parks in California in the early years when his children were small. The amusement parks committed no major error, just dozens of little ones, from lack of cleanliness to indifferent service. When Disneyland opened in 1955, top priority was given to managing the hundreds of little things that create an overall image. In fact, Disney's quality control extended even to the mosquitoes. They were prevented from entering the park by nonstop nocturnal spraying.

The companies winning the image war today are led by individuals with the same fanatical attention to detail shown by Disney. Image is the sum total of all the little things you do. All these small things, taken together, give people a picture of who you are and for what you stand. Building a positive image means applying standards of excellence to everything, small and large. The image winners give attention to the elephants and the mosquitoes. The losers claim to only have time for the elephants.

Any business that wants to succeed today must become

image-conscious. Our modern society requires attention to image. Not so long ago, people lived in one town all their lives. A business person's honesty was judged by personal character alone. People lived with and bought from and sold to generations of the same family. Only strangers were suspect.

There are very few places where those ground rules apply today. We move often and live in neighborhoods where we know few people well. Decisions about who to trust in business can, in most cases, no longer be made by getting to know a person's character over time. Yet, dozens of buying and selling decisions are made every week.

In this atmosphere, little things, external things, take on much greater importance in communicating to others who and what you are. First impressions, those critical first ten seconds, have taken the place of long-term acquaintance in evaluating character and trustworthiness. How you dress and what you drive and what your store or office looks like are all clues hungrily devoured by time-pressed potential buyers trying to decide whether to leave their money with you or with the folks down the street.

The power of the five senses is what makes or breaks that all-important first impression. Whenever the brain encounters "a first", it goes into five-sense overdrive, registering every new sensation. Within a few seconds the brain has collected enough data to form an opinion. That first impression, even though flawed, is cast in stone. In time, a long time, that first impression may change when new information is received, but that first opinion may stay in the background for years. What sense do you think has the strongest influence over this first impression? That's right, the eyes.

THE HIGH STAKES APPEARANCE GAME

Research shows that 83 percent of the decisions we make every day are made with our eyes. We quickly scan a person, place, or thing and decide if we want to do business there or not.

As a result, the importance of appearances has never been greater. For business people, concern with external image has never been more legitimate. In many ways, our fast lane society demands it.

Masterplanning your external image means carefully thinking through the dozens of visual messages you send to the public about who you are and what your business stands for. It means replacing the shoddy images with ones that reflect standards of excellence. It means eliminating mixed messages that confuse the customer.

So many mixed messages in the external image area are being sent from otherwise competent business people that I have stopped being amazed: the owner of a company that manufactures lawn and garden chemicals, whose own lawn is full of crabgrass; the medical doctor who smokes and drinks to excess; the health club with dirty floors and an overweight receptionist.

Some companies do better than others, but then fail to give attention to just one area that detracts from their overall effort. A few years ago I visited the offices of one of America's fastest growing law firms. The building was modern and impressive. the decor in the reception area was very sophisticated and attractive. Right in the middle of it all was an improperly dressed, gum-chewing receptionist who looked like she had not washed her hair in a month. Elephants don't bite; mosquitoes do. And with some, the mosquitoes are eating them alive.

A number of years ago our dentist suggested that our daughter Tracy see an orthodontist for some special dental work. I asked if he could recommend anyone, and he mentioned a new dentist in the area. As we drove into the parking lot on the day of the appointment, I noticed a well-landscaped, attractive building. The office decor was also inviting.

We were ushered into an inner office waiting area. After about ten minutes, a man who appeared to be about twenty-seven years old came down the hall toward us. He had red hair and a red beard, both in need of a trim. He was wearing orange, yellow, and green plaid pants, an orange Izod shirt, and brown earth shoes with crepe soles. My brain immediately went into action and concluded this could not possibly be our dentist. To my surprise, he continued walking in our direction and sat down beside us. Sure enough, this was our man. He immediately launched into a highly technical description of my daughter's dental condition. I had to admit he sounded very knowledge-able, very competent. When he completed his presentation, he said with confidence, "I'll look forward to seeing you in two weeks and we'll get started."

I smiled and shook hands, then steered Tracy straight past the reception desk and out into the parking lot without mak-ing a return appointment. Something was bothering me and I was not sure what it was. Two weeks later it struck me. This young man simply did not fit the image of a dentist that I had in my mind's eye. When I first saw him, my brain did not register "dentist"; it registered "golf caddy." My brain simply could not visualize this "golf caddy" working on my daughter's teeth.

The relationship between personal appearance and success has been well documented through scientific studies. Appropri-ate dress and appearance standards for the professional have been made very clear, yet millions of intelligent people refuse to take these studies seriously. Your ability to attract, keep, per-suade, influence and move clients and customers to action is greatly affected by personal appearance.

The human brain is a fact finding, and decision making de-vice. Therefore the brain is gathering information all the time. Through the help of the five senses your customer is judging your intelligence, your education, your income level and your honesty. The entire process takes about thirty seconds at the most.

Personal appearance is used as a form of self expression and that can be a problem. Many people have taken this art form to the point they could be framed and hung in a museum. Em-ployee appearance remains a nuisance for many. Owners of a business are often judged by the appearance standards they allow to exist. I would suggest this issue be taken seriously, as the image game can be won or lost right here.

The number one reason for the problem of poor employee appearance is lack of understanding. In other words people don't understand either how their grooming affects the perceived image of the whole company or the psychology of personal appearance. If they did understand these realities and dynamics they would not show up to work dressed the way they often do. Often home and educational environment offer young employees few positive examples. And to my knowledge the power of personal appearance is not taught in our schools today. Therefore it is up to the employer to set appearance standards and educate new employees about those standards. Setting an example is part of the job of management, but even a visual walking breathing example is not enough. Put your guidelines in writing and explain all requests carefully along with the reasons for those requests. Most employees will cooperate if they understand the reasons behind your requests. This must be done within the first weeks of employment because talking to someone about personal appearance after time and relationships have formed is one of the hardest jobs human resource professionals must face. In the area of employee appearance it is a well known fact, left to make their own choices on dress, only the most professional employees will chose to exceed the appearance standards of the organization. My office is located on the Pacific Coast Highway in southern California, we are part of an office condominium complex so I share my building with eight small business owners, three art galleries, a stockbroker, an engineer, a printing broker, a sales representative, and a plastic surgeon. All are successful and are men, to see these men come to work in their shorts, golf shirts, and thongs is a lesson in human nature. When given a choice most people will chose casual, simple and comfortable. If you believe judges or ministers covered by robes, or television newscasters sitting behind those desks are perfectly coordinated from head to foot, guess again. Professional grooming and dress is considered an element of common sense by most large companies, so little training and time is given the subject.

Professional dress inspires professional behavior, in other words dress and attitude correlate. To prove my point take an average group of high school students to a restaurant and watch their actions and behavior. Then dress the same group of students for a prom in formal attire, send them to the same restaurant and once again watch their attitudes and behavior. It simply makes good sense for a company to develop a list of dress, grooming, and attitude expectations and then to monitor them on a regular basis.

Ken Matejka, Professor of Management, Duquesne University writes: "People tend to reject events that seem inconsistent with what they perceive and what they believe. They also reject unclear messages and behaviors and any person whose actions and words are inconsistent. These conflicts cause greater inner turmoil and confusion because the receiver doesn't know what to do."

The total Image Masterplan covers all the major elements connected with your external image: product quality, tangible image, advertising, community involvement, and investor and media relations. Each one of these in its own way is absolutely critical to your success.

QUALITY STILL COUNTS

The single most important factor affecting your long-term business image and reputation is product quality. The key to product quality, as shown in some of America's recent business success stories, is listening to the customer.

When GM shortened the new Cadillac by two feet in 1984, drivers thumbed their noses and sales plummeted. Instead of increasing the advertising budget to try to gain public acceptance, GM asked their customers for help. They asked fifteen hundred Cadillac owners for their repeated input on the design of new models over a three-year period. The GM engineers took notes while these people climbed into prototypes and gave them critical feedback. As a result, when the longer, flashier De-Ville and Fleetwood models hit the showrooms, sales jumped 36 percent and have shown no sign of slackening. Product quality means listening to the customer.

Techsonic Industries of Eufaula, Alabama, which makes the Humminbird depth finder, has discovered the same thing. Depth finders are electronic devices used by boat fishermen to measure water depth and help track fish. In a classic example of success through perseverance, Techsonic endured the failure of nine new products in a row prior to 1985. That was when Chairman James Balcom decided to interview twenty-five sportsmen's groups across the country to find out exactly what they wanted in a depth finder. The year after the newly designed model hit the market, sales tripled to $80 million. Balcom gave credit where it was due: "The customer literally developed the product for us."

Techsonic is also an example of the way in which a company's philosophy and motto can be a key to their success. Their motto? "The quality of any product or service is what the customer says it is."

For most of you, product quality is a foregone conclusion. No amount of lavish public relations or customer service will make up for poor product quality. I overheard a quote attributed to a top executive at one of the big three American auto manufacturers, "We're not in the business of making cars; we're in the business of making money." The Japanese must have been listening, and learning. My slogan "Never sacrifice long term image for short-term profits" or put another way, "Never sacrifice product quality for short term revenues" should have been emblazoned across the executive's forehead.

Advertising may bring the customer in, but just how long will the image created by advertising last if the customer is not totally satisfied with your product and the quality of service rendered? Can you sincerely offer an unconditional 100 percent money back guarantee and mean it? No amount of well-financed imagizing can make up for a product which is less than your customers expect.

There is no doubt that it takes more than imagining the externals to win in business. It takes a quality product and a lot of hard work. It is also true that if you fail to give attention to external image in today's competitive world, you are guaranteed to fail. That was brought home to me as a group of veteran buyers for a major department store chain listened to a presentation by a young man on the youth-renewing benefits of his new cosmetic line. Within five minutes the group was fidgeting. The senior buyer from New York cut in. "No offense, sir," he said, "but you can cut the reading of the ingredients. Just show us how it's packaged." Both product quality *and* visual image are essential to long-term success.

YOUR SENSORY REPORT CARD

The tangible image areas we detect with our five senses include everything from logo to location. Your company name and logo are two highly visible elements in your image system. It is worth spending the time and money up front to create the most effective package possible in these areas. This is especially true for new entrepreneurial businesses.

Your name and logo communicate who you are to the public. Both name and logo should accurately capture what you are about.

Names have visual impact. The shorter the name, the greater its impact. The name should be memorable, as well. American business recognizes corporate names to be so important that more than one thousand established companies change their names every year, with the help of an entire cottage industry of professional "name changers."

I make a game of looking at the name of a small walk-in business and trying to figure out what it does or sells. Many of the names are clever, but do not convey what product or service they provide. Take a look at the following list, and see if you can figure out what these businesses do:

- The Carved Horse
- Duck Soup
- Flamingo Fantasy
- George's
- Just Clever
- Something More
- Manufacturing Unlimited

The Carved Horse sounds like a toy store, Duck Soup like a restaurant, Flamingo Fantasy a cocktail lounge and George's . . . well, who knows? The truth is that all of these are clothing stores. Thieve's Market, McGee and Me, and Johnston and Murphy are all shoe stores. Compare these names with Foot Locker, Ken's Bootery, or Leed's Shoes. Who would you give an A to for intelligent naming? You know what the last group sells without having to ask. Make it as clear as possible what service or product you supply through your name. My favorite florist is simply named "Flowers."

Your external image must communicate clearly and attractively who you are. It also should reinforce that image over and over, without sending mixed messages. Your corporate name and logo should be reflected in your signage, in your letterhead and business cards, in your product packaging, in everything that represents you to the public. Your image statements must be unified for maximum impact.

The Power of Place

The location of your business is itself an important image consideration. Depending on your market, the image of one city may be more appropriate than another. If walk-in business is not a consideration and a more upscale image would be of benefit, you can always rent a post office box in a nearby neighborhood or city with a more prestigious address. The inclusion of a FAX number on your business card and letterhead is fast becoming an image essential as well. If owning one is not an option, make arrangements with an establishment that offers publicly accessible facsimile machines.

Building location and maintenance are absolutely critical if your customers come to you. You need to ask yourself what kind of image statement is made if you are located in a run-down strip mall with half the shops vacant.

You want to be viewed as successful, right? All other things being equal, most people would rather deal with a successful business person than an unsuccessful one. Your business may be doing well itself, but if you are surrounded by poorly maintained or vacant shops, the "failure" image attaches itself to you nonetheless.

You have heard that the three most important elements in opening a new business are location, location, and location. If you open your business on a street that is poorly maintained, has very light traffic, or is surrounded by vacant shops, the image of failure will precede your opening.

My consulting work recently took me to one of America's largest real estate franchise corporations. Although this company is successful in many ways, their image is handicapped by an almost total neglect of attention to corporate standards, other than the money spent on national advertising. No standards have been set for the visual quality of their franchise offices across the country. There is no uniform interior decor beyond the logo and the color scheme of the career apparel. Their image varies drastically from city to city, even from office to office in the same city.

This oversight could have a serious impact on the company's bottom line. Their high budget national television advertising campaign will actually begin to work against them as the public compares the shoddy image of the real estate office in their town to the polished image projected on their television screens.

The Power of Color
Colors generate emotion. That is why even the color scheme of your office decor needs to be intelligently thought through.

Would you spend a million dollars to build an exclusive restaurant and then paint it and everything in it black? "No one's that stupid," you say. Maybe not. I know of an expensive restaurant with a black and white color scheme that opened not long ago near my home in southern California. It promptly began losing money hand over fist.

I consulted with a major sports complex and found bright pink carpet in the men's weight room. My dentist, who is otherwise a very intelligent man, decorated his waiting area in red, white, and blue. Anyone who has studied the psychology of color knows that red is an exciting color that speeds the pulse and raises the blood pressure. Red does not create a soothing atmosphere, particularly for those who are petrified before they enter the waiting room.

While working with Ice Capades, I visited one of their newly opened skating rinks. As we walked up to the building, I asked the manager about the pluses and minuses of the skating rink business.

"Probably our number-one image problem," he said, "has to do with the cold. No matter how much fun this sport is, some people just do not like fighting the cold temperatures in our rinks."

As I entered the beautiful facility, my eyes were instantly drawn to a stunning sculpture that dominated the entire back wall. Made of stainless steel, it was intertwined with shades of purple and blue. It beautifully captured the feel of ice and snow, and as I studied it, I involuntarily shivered.

Turning to my client I said, "that is a gorgeous sculpture. But I don't think it's helping you with your number-one image problem"

The sculptor was obviously a true artist. The company had the right idea in trying to decorate to reflect the theme of its rink. But a lack of insight on the psychology of color was actually handicapping its business.

If a professional interior decorator is not a possibility, perhaps a knowledgeable friend can help. In any case, you should never underestimate the powerful effect on your business of the visual image of your building, its landscaping, and its interior decor.

Pay Attention To All the Senses

Walt Disney raised the use of the five senses to an art form. The Disney theme parks are a total sensory experience from the moment you drive into the landscaped parking lot. Cheerful music fills the air at the front gate, and you sense your mood changing before you have purchased your tickets. As soon as you go through the gates your nose picks up the aroma of popcorn from the vendor on Town Square. Then you are on to Main Street, where a band oom-pahs your mood up another notch. As you walk down Main Street, you are treated to the delicious smells from the chocolate confectioneries because the vents were deliberately directed out toward the street instead of into the sky.

The total sensory approach can be used effectively in a professional context as well. One of the most successful dentists anywhere is Dr. Ron Bentham of Penticton, Canada. He is successful not only because he is competent and thoroughly professional, but also because he has created an effective image for his business through the creative use of the five senses.

What is the number-one image problem for dentists today? The fear factor. We are afraid to go to the dentist, afraid of the pain. Dr. Bentham designed an office that people would enjoy coming to, where the atmosphere itself would reduce anxiety levels. First, the office building resembles a lovely country house, surrounded by two acres of beautiful landscaping and trees.

The inside does not look like the usual sterile dentist office either. Dr. Bentham used a bit of architectural psychology in the layout. Reasoning that the kitchen is the least threatening room in a home and the place where guests tend to naturally gather, the first room his client walks into is a combination kitchen and reception area. The scent of freshly baked bread fills the room. The new arrival is offered a muffin and a cup of coffee by Mrs. Bentham, who always keeps a batch baking during office hours. If a person prefers, he or she can wait in an adjoining living room area. There are no reception room chairs here, only couches that continue the country ambience.

After finishing the refreshments, the patient is given a toothbrush with which to brush his or her teeth before being taken to the examining room. Tall windows with a view of the landscaping dominate the room and offset the presence of the normally intimidating equipment hanging over the chair.

In addition, the staff has been instructed to say at least two nice things to every patient who comes in, something that connects emotionally and makes the patient feel good. Is it any wonder that Dr. Bentham has a long patient waiting list, has been featured on the local television news show, and is one of the few dentists in the world where patients deliberately come early to appointments? He has captured the power of the total sensory dimension of image making.

By contrast, I have worked with another dentist who is very competent and personally likeable. However, his building is old, and you have to walk by vacant offices to get to his, which features an old-fashioned decor. Despite my advice, he refused to spend the money to get a new office. As a result, he has made a decision to permanently exile himself to a lower level of success than he could achieve with an improved image.

The wraparound sensory approach to imagizing can work for any type of business, even an auto repair shop. After working through an Image Masterplan, the owner of an auto repair shop now keeps an immaculate work area, spray cleans the outside of the car with water and the inside with scent after the repair is completed, and ties a lollypop and thank you note to the steering wheel! What was this shop like before? It was like hundreds of other auto repair shops; dirty and disorganized; the mechanics wore uniforms covered with grease and oil, and a car never left there without its share of greasy finger prints. Sensory imagizing does not have to be a high budget affair.

Are you beginning to get the idea that imagizing can work for anybody? It can! It does not matter whether you are a large multinational corporation or a corner business with one location, projecting a positive image is going to make a difference to your bottom line. Plain and simple, one of the key ingredients to making more money is improving your image. In fact, for smaller businesses it is less complicated and less expensive to improve your image. There is no extensive bureaucracy that can distort the image you want to deliver.

The image changes you make, though, should not be arbitrary or hit and miss. They should flow out of the image analysis in your Masterplan. Identify your weak areas and address the problems you discover. Remember, your external image is the portion of your Image Masterplan that people see, taste, hear, smell, and touch. The Image Masterplan, then, is targeted to address these specific areas.

The hospital industry in America today is facing major financial challenges. Costs are spiraling, and more and more people are opting to be treated on an outpatient basis.

My counsel to hospital administrators has been to change their whole corporate philosophy. Instead of a negative, "treat-your-illness" approach, hospitals need to be able to say, "We're in the health business!" This philosophy can be reinforced with a number of external image changes, such as creating an atmosphere of a hotel lobby in the reception area and adding a bakery/restaurant featuring healthy food. The aroma of freshly baked breads would greet those arriving in the lobby, rather than the smell of antiseptic. The hospital gift shop could feature quality products for a reasonable price, made by the members of the hospital auxiliary. A whole new retail image could be encouraged with the addition of a drive-up window for the bakery and separate outside entrances for the restaurant and the gift shop.

The key in this, and any other imagining process, is to think more creatively about what you can do to meet your customers' needs and to help them have a more pleasant experience.

WHAT ABOUT ADVERTISING?

Advertising is the primary way the public is introduced to a new product or service. Some forms of advertising wield powerful images; others do not. Grey Poupon did not just advertise, they imagized their mustard as the mustard of the elite. Fancy Feast did the same thing with cat food.

As never before, reality is being served to the world in blips and bites. Television's ninety-second "news blips" and fifteen-second "sound bites" have revolutionized the way we learn in the twentieth century. Over the last forty years, we have evolved from a society of readers to a society of viewers.

A large percentage of our judgments about people and products are now formed on the basis of visual imagery, symbols, and concise, carefully crafted summaries. In this context, advertising, both print and electronic, has been elevated to the level of a science, with enormously high stakes. The challenge for today's advertiser is the competition. The sheer volume of product information blitzing the consumer is staggering.

Fifty-seven percent of the world's advertising is done in the United States. Between the morning newspaper, the car radio, the roadside billboards, the evening television, and the magazines on the coffee table, the average American city dweller is bombarded by more than two hundred and fifty commercial messages a day. Most of these are screened out, with only the most effective actually penetrating and making an impact.

In today's white-hot competitive atmosphere, your advertising needs should be entrusted to professionals. Even if you are planning a local newspaper ad or direct mail flier, an amateur piece cannot hope to compete effectively for the consumer's attention with the other two hundred and forty-nine professional commercial messages.

Stand Out From The Crowd

Although you rely on professionals to produce your advertising, you do have a responsibility to give intelligent direction to

the designer of your advertising. Primary among these responsibilities is the need to ensure that the advertising accurately cap-
tures your uniqueness, that aspect of your business or product
that is different than or superior to your competition.

It is essential that your advertising campaign not be isolated
from the rest of your image program, but rather be unified with
it. A single theme, a single image slogan, should run through
your entire Image Masterplan. This, of course, means that you
have completed your mission statement, your philosophy statement, your written version of your long term goals, and your
analysis of your number-one image problem. These give the
professionals the direction they need and protects you from
image backlash by ensuring that the advertising represents you
and your product.

The ads that penetrate today are not only professionally produced, but designed to emotionally connect as well. Not all advertising agencies understand this, and you should carefully
evaluate their other work before hiring them.

Take the McDonalds-Burger King advertising strategy, for instance. Burger King totally missed the point by hammering on
the "McDonalds fries and we broil" theme. Their advertising
focused on the competition and a fact, instead of focusing on
the consumers. Burger King failed in that campaign to make
that important emotional connection. Meanwhile, McDonalds
refused to be baited and continued to strike emotional chords:
images of kids and fun and lonely grandfather types meeting
lonely grandmother types to share their hamburgers.

The advertising war between Pepsi and Coke is very interesting. No war can compare with the hype of the "cola wars." Powerful celebrity endorsements is a major element of the war.
Super Bowl XXIV had us watching tennis star Chris Evert drink-
ing coke. Michael J. Fox, television and motion-picture star, goes
to great trouble to obtain a Pepsi. Super Bowl XXV continued
the war with the spoils going to Pepsi.

On and on it goes. Each time one company comes out with
a new advertising campaign, it is not long before you see a

rebuttal ad from the other camp. Again, they are focusing on one another, rather than on the consumer. Why isn't a larger portion of their advertising budgets diverted to community relations where they would receive positive media through what they give back to the community?

Imagine a can of Coke or Pepsi against a deep blue background. Then these words appear:

We have chosen to donate the money we would normally spend on a commercial production to the following:

- The New Orleans Children's Hospital
- The Drug Rehabilitation Center in San Francisco
- The Muscular Dystrophy Association in Denver

What do they do instead? They spend millions of dollars targeting and attacking each other instead of focusing on the consumers, their communities.

The remarkable thing about the cola wars is that Coke at one time was striking chords within our hearts. I will never forget the ad of a few years ago featuring Mean Joe Green. It shows Joe trudging off the field, dejected and alone. A little boy is waiting for him in the tunnel leading to the locker rooms, waiting with a Coke in his hand. Without a word the boy offers Joe his Coke. As the ad closes, Joe strips off his jersey and gives it to the little boy. This is a powerful ad because it connects emotionally with the viewer.

You may not have a high-powered national TV advertising campaign, but you need to ensure that the advertising dollars you are spending are maximized by including the emotional connection to the customer.

Do not just advertise, imagize. After your Masterplan is complete, your image comfort zone will be established. Customize your advertising to the comfort zone of the market you want to reach. Consider not only the facts but ego, self-image, and comfort of the customer you want to reach.

Smart Charity

A northern California newspaper recently carried the following headline: "It's Surprising What Charitable Giving Does to One's Image." I never expected to see an Image Masterplan statement on the sports page, but there it was. The article went on to tell the story of professional golfer Scott Hoch, who had lost the 1989 Masters Golf Tournament the month before by missing a 30-inch putt. Overnight, Hoch became the butt of every golf joke told on links across the country. "How can anyone miss a 30-inch putt?" the fans snickered. Hoch seemed destined to go down in history next to Wrong-Way Corrigan and other classics of ineptitude.

Three weeks later, still the butt of jokes, he won the Las Vegas Invitational. But it was not the win that grabbed the headlines and turned Scott Hoch's image around. It was what he did after the win. He announced that he would donate $100,000 of his winning purse to the Orlando Regional Medical Center. As one sports commentator put it, "How can you not like a guy like this, one who has suffered a devastating loss, recovers to win, and then exhibits a remarkable generosity?"

Even more than a winner, everybody loves a giver. No single act can so effectively turn around a failing image as a skillfully placed gift to charity.

The key phrase here, as it relates to image building, is "skillfully placed." There are many worthy causes that need support in our society. A large number of us contribute to a great many of them quietly and without any fanfare. But as a business person, certain of your contributions should be designated to serve two needs: the charity itself, and the positioning of your image in the community. It is these latter contributions that need to be skillfully placed.

I recommend three basic criteria for a skillfully placed charitable gift. The gift should be given to a specific, identifiable project, as opposed to an amorphous, multi-project fund drive. That is not to say that such fund drives should not be supported, but your image-related giving should be to specific, individual projects in the community where you can more easily be identified as the patron of that charity.

Second, the gift should be to a charity or cause with an emotional connection to the community. McDonalds has shown great skill in this regard with its support of the Special Olympics and its establishment of the Ronald McDonald Houses for the families of seriously ill children. More than a hundred of the houses have been built by McDonalds worldwide at a cost of millions. The return on the investment in terms of enhanced image has been enormous, because McDonalds gives to causes the public feels deeply about. IBM and Apple have shown similar astuteness in their donations of computers to public schools across the country.

The third criteria for skillful community giving is the gift should be accompanied by maximum media exposure. For Scott Hoch to announce his $100,000 gift to the Children's Hospital while in the winner's spotlight demonstrated a savvy media awareness.

The Loggers Association in the Pacific Northwest has identified its number-one image problem. Loggers know that many people see them as anti-environmentalists involved in the raping of America's forest land. "Just the opposite is true," the loggers told me. "We love the forests. That's why we work in them and from them. One of the key issues facing us today is the replanting of trees." Among other things, I advised them to take some of the timber they cut, identify some widows or other needy families in the community, and donate the wood and their own time to fix up the houses of these people and in the process, get media coverage from the local newspapers. These simple but emotional gestures of service in a community do more for the image of a organization than anything else.

What about smaller companies? Does community giving have to involve millions of dollars to affect one's image? Not at all, as Texas financier T. Boone Pickens discovered. Pickens, wanting to improve his community image in Amarillo, donated one million dollars to a local college. But he received little public response to the gift, so he called in an outside consultant to advise him. The consultant told him, "The *smart* money gives in a way that will touch people." He told Pickens that the donations do not have to be enormous, just intelligently placed. He recommended that Pickens buy the lettermen's jackets for the athletic teams at a local high school. Pickens did, for total outlay of only thirty thousand dollars, a comparatively small sum. The response was overwhelming media coverage, letters from parents and students and a far greater response than to his million dollar gift.

THINK "MEDIA"

Media relations in general are an important part of building a solid community image. You do not have to be involved in charitable giving to get positive coverage from the media. You simply need to cultivate some media relationships and periodically supply them with press releases and other information they can use. Once you begin to "think media" you will become aware of innumerable subjects appropriate for press releases. You can:

- Tie in your business with news events of the day.
- Conduct a poll or survey and release the results.
- Issue a report.
- Make an analysis or prediction about local or national business issue.
- Announce a new appointment or promotion.
- Celebrate an anniversary.
- Make an award.
- Hold a contest.
- Pass a resolution.
- Stage, or co-sponsor, a community event.
- Make a trip.
- Appear before public bodies.
- Tie into a well-known day or week.
- Organize a tour.
- Adapt a national report or survey for local use.

The possibilities are only limited by your imagination. The free publicity that results cannot be bought at any price.

Your corporate credo should be: Customers first, employees second, the community third, and investors fourth. If you have done your image work in the other key areas, including building a reputation as an involved member of your community, your task with investor and shareholder relations is made much easier. It is then a matter of frequent communication and occasional personal contact.

Experienced investors are looking for companies with a proven track record and a positive image on the front lines. That is where the majority of your attention should be directed. Send investors and key shareholders carefully packaged summaries of your achievements as a company and the image-building projects you have created in your community. They are looking for return on investment and evidence of a company they can be proud to be involved with.

THE ROLE OF PERSONAL IMAGE

External image, especially visual image, touches every aspect of your business. Your brochures, your business cards, your print and electronic advertising, your office, your desk, your spouse, your briefcase, your receptionist, your parking lot, your building, your clothes, everything that is visually connected with your business eventually affects your income. You are in the center of it all.

To implement a major image engineering job on your business and not show the same concern for your own personal image is simply foolish. There are unwritten personal image rules in corporate America. Those who consistently follow them win; those who do not lose.

It is amazing that, with the number of books that address this subject, there are still college graduates who show up for interviews in jeans and CEOs with short socks and ties that do not come close to their belt buckle.

People are constantly evaluating you, looking for clues about your competence, by looking at your "second skins," the things you surround yourself with your clothes, your car, your weight. The sales you close and the promotions you earn may have more to do with your personal image than you realize.

At the age of twenty-one, I opened my first business with one of my college professors as my silent partner. Not long into the new venture we needed the services of an attorney. My partner suggested someone she knew in a nearby city. The mention of that particular city raised a red flag with me. The community had had a low-income reputation for many years.

My concerns grew as we drove through run-down neighborhoods to reach the attorney's office, but I was determined to keep an open mind. The battle was over when he greeted us wearing an out-of-date suit, sat down, crossed his legs, and revealed a big hole in the sole of his shoe. From that moment on I did not hear a word he said. I just kept thinking that if this professional man was so broke that he could not afford a decent suit or a new pair of shoes, then he must not be a very successful attorney. We left and never returned.

The key to success in maintaining a positive image in the public's mind is a mentality of zealous dedication to standards of excellence in everything you do and everything you surround yourself with. It is not an easy path to take. But it is the only one that will lead to the long-term satisfactions of a sterling image and reputation and financial security.

5

Your Internal Image
The Hidden Half

The image employees have of their company, the internal image, is the most undervalued aspect of the business image equation. While a positive external image, the image that the public holds, wins you the right to be heard, it is the crucial area of internal image that determines whether you have anything worthwhile to say once the customer is listening. These two halves of the image equation center around two different "critical events."

The critical event of the external image process is getting the customer in the front door. If the customer enters and finds a positive environment, then your external image programs have accomplished what you intended. At this point the baton passes to your internal image to complete the transaction.

The second critical event is the "moment of truth" when your potential customer first comes in contact with you or your front-line staff and decides on the basis of how he or she is treated how well your perceived public image matches your reality. That critical event determines whether the customer is won or lost.

How often have you gone into a store or place of business whose advertising proclaims "the customer is king?" You might think, "At last, a business that will appreciate me as a customer." You walk through the door and find the surroundings beautiful: "This business certainly has spent money to impress me with their interior. And they've succeeded." You find what you want, and you are ready to make a purchase. You go to the cash register and there are two or three employees talking about their dates last night or domestic problems or anything else other than business. Come to think of it, where were they when you were looking for the item you wanted. Nobody has treated you like a king, or even a prince. This business has failed the moment of truth.

Of the two, external image is the easier to change, and the key to initially opening the door of opportunity. Internal image, on the other hand, is harder to change, but much more important to your long-term success and reputation. Employee loyalty for the company and enthusiasm for customer service are at the heart of that internal image.

Employee Loyalty?

It has been my experience that most employees have no idea of the influence they have over the customers' perception of their company. I once pulled into a service station near my home and asked the young man at the pumps to fill my tank. He did so, filled out my credit card slip, and handed me my bill.

Shocked at the total, I turned back to the attendant and said, "Good grief, the gas in this station is expensive!" I expected him to reassure me about providing a higher quality of service for that price, or some such response. Instead, he said, "I know. Ain't that awful? I don't even buy my own gas here!" Needless to say, I never went back.

A few years ago, my company used the services of one printer exclusively. They had always done a good job for us, and we never had any reason to change. Diane was the delivery person for the printer, and over a period of time my office staff and I got to know her fairly well. As Diane became more comfortable around us, she began to share criticisms of her company with us. In fact, Diane rarely had anything positive to say about her boss.

Eventually, based solely on Diane's gossip and complaints, I became convinced that there was something terribly wrong with her company, even though they continued to serve our needs satisfactorily. I finally changed printers. Evidently, so did a number of other customers. One day not long after that, Diane stopped in to tell us she no longer had a job. The printing company had lost so many customers that it was having to lay off employees. Was Diane bitter about the situation? She certainly was, although she had no idea that it was her own fault to some degree.

My advice to employees is simple: either represent your employer positively to the public or quit and find a company for which you can be proud to work. This advice is for all employees at all levels, whether you work in the mail room or board room or drive a truck.

Critical comments to customers amount to nothing more than biting the hand that feeds you. Your company cannot remain financially strong without a positive, motivated staff. As the company's position is weakened, so your own financial security as employees is weakened.

Internal image, then, is the image of the company among the employees, and the image of the company that is projected by the employees to customers. Put simply, *a negative internal image will inevitably mean lost customers and a negative reputation.* Although it is not easy to correct a soured internal image, it is certainly less expensive than finding new customers. Research by the Boston consulting firm Forum Corporation indicates that keeping a customer typically costs only one-fifth as much as acquiring a new one.

Not even the most successful companies can afford to overlook the importance of internal image and employee morale. In the book by Douglas Smith and Robert Alexander *Fumbling the Future: How Xerox Invented, then Ignored, the First Personal Computer* there is a description of how Xerox brought together some of the most respected names in computer science in 1970 and gave them a mandate to invent the industry's first personal computer. The group was fabulously successful, developing such innovations as computer icons, mice, and local area networks. But personality conflicts and corporate infighting eventually broke the Palo Alto team apart. It was left to Apple Computers to establish early dominance in the personal computer field. Teamwork and employee morale can determine whether a company with a great idea and a lot of talent becomes a long-term success or just a footnote in history.

THE RED FLAGS OF MORALE

Because employee morale is so significant for a positive image, an effective manager must constantly have his or her finger on the pulse of the work force, looking for early signs of trouble. Any of the following should be viewed as red flags.

(1) *Output.* A sudden drop in the quality or quantity of work, without apparent reason, is a danger signal.

(2) *Friction.* Bickering and fighting among employees may be caused by dissatisfaction and poor morale.

(3) *Absenteeism and Lateness.* When otherwise punctual and steady workers come in late or stay out often, it may be a symptom of dissatisfaction.

(4) *Turnover.* When employees quit or ask for transfers, you should try to find the real cause. The first answer given may not be the real one; in-depth probing may be needed.

(5) *Reaction to Order-Giving.* When you meet significant resistance, when you have to repeat orders over and over again, or when you find yourself taking disciplinary action more often than normal, you will almost always find low morale as the cause.

(6) *Complaints and Suggestions.* When suggestions dry up, it is often a sign that morale is poor. Disgruntled workers do not care enough about their jobs to offer ideas for improvement. You also need to look at the type of complaints you are getting. Are they petty—the kind made by irritable and dissatisfied people—or are they legitimate concerns?

What about specific training in customer relations? Is it important to train your employees how to work effectively with the customer and how to give outstanding service? Absolutely. I will discuss that later in this chapter. However, that kind of "how to" training is useless without the development of healthy employee attitudes. As American Express executive Tommaso Zanzotto says: "When we want to increase customer satisfaction, technical training how to write a letter to a card member, for example is easy. The quantum leap comes from improving employees' attitudes."

In fact, training employees in customer relations without also working on employee attitudes and morale is a lot like putting the proverbial gold ring in a pig's snout: it looks ridiculous. I was staying at a major San Francisco hotel recently, and all the staff I came in contact with seemed to have poor attitudes. The porter that carried my luggage to my room was glum and uncommunicative; the room service personnel were noticeably abrupt and performed only the minimum required.

During my stay, I noticed on the lapels of all the staff a button with the words "Sevens Are Heaven." I finally asked one of the employees the meaning of the button. He explained that it had to do with a new customer relations training program launched by corporate headquarters. Each hotel guest was encouraged to fill out a card rating the quality of service performed by the staff. "Seven" was the highest rating on these cards, thus the "Sevens Are Heaven" button.

The irony of the situation was incredible: staff with obvious attitude problems openly advertising their new customer relations program! I have seen similar wasted efforts in many companies: corporate headquarters decides to impose a top-down program aimed at improved customer relations in a local situation characterized by low employee morale. It never works. The morale must be addressed first.

EMPLOYEES AS CUSTOMERS/
MOTIVATION ON THE INSIDE

How do you improve employee morale and generate the high level of motivation essential to your long-term success, reputation, and image? There is always the heavy-handed approach. As in the now famous humorous employee sign that you see on office walls. The sign reads: "FIRINGS WILL CONTINUE UNTIL MORALE IMPROVES." Even though the sign is obviously funny it is actually not far from many of the management attitudes prevalent throughout American businesses.

The confrontational, adversarial style of management is almost always inappropriate and actually harmful to employee morale in the long run. The way skillful managers achieve high employee morale and employee loyalty is exactly the same way you achieve customer satisfaction and loyalty: by meeting human needs.

In fact, you should try to think of employees as just a different kind of customer: there are external customers, the buyers, and internal customers, the staff. It is essential that both employees and customers be treated with equal consideration and respect. The result will be sky-high motivation among employees and increased satisfaction among buyers. That has been the result for PepsiCo, consistently ranked among the ten most respected companies in America in Fortune's annual survey. Said PepsiCo CEO D. Wayne Calloway: "We have a great team spirit. Our people want to be the Marines. They want to be the finest. We hire eagles and teach them to fly in formation."

A high level of motivation only develops as a company adopts a revolutionary new management philosophy that meeting employees' human and emotional needs is the key to developing employee morale and loyalty. Employee morale and loyalty, in turn, are the keys to a positive internal image with the customers. Employees who feel good about their company and their job will be full of energy. That energy will translate to a friendly and positive attitude toward customers.

What are the human and emotional needs that most need to

be met among employees? There are many, but after surveying thousands of employees in virtually every major industry in the country, I have identified eight needs that are essential. These eight must be met if a motivated work force is to be created.

(1) Employees need vision and a sense of pride in their company.
(2) They need respect from management and a non-adversarial and egalitarian relationship with their bosses.
(3) They need clear, two-way communication with management.
(4) Employees need the opportunity to be creative and to make a unique contribution.
(5) Employees need to be appreciated.
(6) They need recognition for jobs that are done especially well.
(7) Employees need opportunity for advancement.
(8) And a very important employee need is to feel cared for as a human being, not just as a unit of productivity.

In other words, your employees have many of the same needs as your customers. When you treat your customers like human beings, when you make your customers feel important, you create loyal customers. When you treat your employees with dignity and respect, you create loyal, motivated employees who represent your company enthusiastically to the public.

The Need for Vision

Perhaps no need among employees is more important to the development of high morale and company loyalty than the need for vision. Employees need to know where the company is headed and to what high standards it is committed. One of the key responsibilities of management is to instill the company vision continuously.

James Houghton, the CEO of Corning Glass Works, is a model of how to communicate a leader's vision. Houghton makes forty to fifty trips a year to his far-flung divisions, preaching his gospel of product quality. He also requires all new employees to take courses that emphasize the company's high standards and goals. Many companies with a strong internal image have similar orientation programs for new employees.

If you are the owner of a small business, I recommend that, at the very least, you take new employees to lunch and share with them goals you hope to achieve, the history of your company, and the standards to which you are committed. All of this is essential to the development of employees' pride in your company.

Related to this is the increased morale that comes from belonging to a company that has high standards for employee appearance and conduct. As I have already discussed, appearance standards are essential to the development of a positive business image. These standards should be stated immediately and in a manual that is given to all prospective employees at the time they apply for a job. Applicants who do not want to meet your standards for appearance or conduct can then look elsewhere for employment. Those who accept a job are agreeing to uphold your standards.

Some managers express fear that if they establish and enforce high standards for employee appearance and conduct it might contribute to their labor shortage. In fact, the opposite is true. The very fact that a company is selective in who it hires and enforces high standards, increases the attractiveness of the company in the eyes of prospective employees. It certainly increases the esprit de corps of those who work there.

Having definite appearance and conduct standards in writing makes it easier to deal with problem cases later on. I have been asked by clients to deal with employees with odor problems, for instance, simply because the manager did not know how to broach the subject. A written standards manual can help pave the way for these types of conversations.

In addition to a standards manual, which deals with appearance, ethics, and etiquette, every company should also have a policy manual, which explains the factual side of business procedures.

In fact, the best scenario when beginning a new company is to have a standards, policy, and procedure manual available even before the first employee is hired. Doing this will enhance the image of the company and save hours of time in the future trying to solve employee relations problems. All of us know how boring most manuals are so it is important to write this set of guidelines in a positive style and tone. People tend to rebel when they are barraged with rules and things they cannot do. For example a manual may have language that says all employees must take their vacations during a certain time. A more positive approach would be language that invites employees to take their vacation during the summer months because the company wants to encourage employees to enjoy the summer months. When a brief, positive booklet includes a few pertinent cartoons it will be more inviting and more likely to be read. Having new employees read this manual will unexpectedly challenge the people who want to work for a company with standards and vision from those who do not want to rise to that challenge. Providing this booklet is another one of those little things that contribute to a positive image in the future even though it seems like a lot of work early in a company's life.

The Need for Respect

The best-managed companies in America today meet another important need of their employees: the need for respect. In one way or another, each of these successful companies has eliminated the "us-them" barrier between managers and employees that exists in many rigidly hierarchical American corporations.

Honda's American operation, for example, has radically swept away traditional managerial perks in an effort to create an atmosphere of equality. There are no reserved parking places. Everyone eats in the same cafeteria. Executives and workers all wear the same white uniforms. Beyond these symbolic gestures, Honda encourages its workers to participate in decisions that would normally be left to management, like the scheduling of overtime or the rotation of jobs.

Does egalitarianism foster loyalty to the company? Without a doubt. In fact, many Honda employees express a deep bonding with the company. As one American in Honda's body-stamping shop put it, "For once in my life, I've got something to believe in."

Whatever form it takes, the common denominator is respect. At Domino's Pizza, for instance, employees treat one another like customers. To ensure this standard, Domino's sixteen regional offices regularly rate the corporate staff on the quality of service they receive from headquarters. To put teeth into the policy, the monthly bonuses earned by headquarters executives depend on the scores they receive in these evaluations.

At the very least, effective managers should avoid critical confrontations with employees. Respect, and along with it, employee morale, deteriorate rapidly under adversarial conditions. In a recent survey by Robert Half International, one hundred managers were asked what they considered to be the worst breach of business etiquette. First place among responses, cited by 45 percent of the managers, was "Criticizing a subordinate in front of others." Successful managers are increasingly realizing that an atmosphere of mutual respect and equality produces a more highly motivated work force than top-down authoritarianism.

The Need for Communication

One of the most strongly felt needs expressed by employees across the country is the need for better corporate communications. When I surveyed the employees of a major financial institution, number one on their list of complaints was poor communication and the sense of disrespect it created. When employees are brought into the communication loop and kept informed, they feel valued and trusted. This, in turn, helps them feel good about the company.

Good corporate communication involves more than dispensing a regular flow of information. It also involves listening and personal contact. Honda executives, for instance, take a fifteen-hour walking tour of their Ohio plants every two months to personally listen to the ideas of employees who have made the best suggestions for improvement. Executive Vice President Toshi Amino, "If you really want teamwork and good communications, it's time consuming."

The Need to Contribute Creatively

Closely related to the need for good two-way communication is the need for creativity and the opportunity to make a unique contribution. We all see ourselves as possessing unique talents and insights, of being special and individual. When we have the chance to express our creativity in our work, it feeds the need we all have to feel important. No one who feels like an anonymous cog in a wheel will maintain high morale. We need to be given the opportunity to make our own contribution.

One of the most motivated employees I have ever met is a woman bank teller in charge of the drive-up window. Noticing how bored her customers seemed to be while waiting in line in their cars, this woman took the initiative to add a little spice to their day. For those customers who pulled up with dogs in their cars, she shot them a doggy biscuit along with their canister of money or receipts. For harried-looking mothers with cars full of pre-schoolers, she dropped stickers for the children's hands in the tube. When management learned of her unorthodox transactions, they wisely allowed her to continue not only because of all the delighted customers, but also because of how motivated this woman had become about her job.

If you allow employees to make unique contributions in even small ways, their morale will be greatly improved. Conversely, high-control bosses who assume they are the only ones with good ideas are usually running departments with under-motivated, unhappy employees.

3M is a U. S. company with high marks for encouraging creativity among its workers. As a result, 3M now has fifty thousand products in circulation, ranging from the highly successful Post-it notes to bioelectronic ears for the hearing-impaired.

Asked to explain the company's success, one outside analyst, Theresa Gusman of Salomon Brothers, said, "3M gives people an environment in which they can create, and they just come up with brilliant idea after brilliant idea." Allowing employees to make their own creative contribution is good business. Bad business is stifling their creativity.

When a customer takes the time to call, write, or otherwise inform you of an idea or problem, you take the time to listen. Give the same respect and courtesy to your employees. It will certainly pay off in amazing ways. Stop for a moment and think: would you rather have a happy employee talking with your customers or one who is harboring resentment? It just makes good business sense.

The Need for Appreciation

Recently, one company I had previously worked with lost a top-notch, twenty-year veteran employee. She had worked her way to the top of her department over twenty-nine other people through hard work and consistent sacrifice for the company, like giving up a vacation when it threatened the completion of a project. When she was transferred to the company's overseas division for one year, she was promised her job as department head would be saved for her.

To her shock, when she returned a year later, she was told she could have a position in that department again, but not as department head. In fact, she would have to report to someone who had previously been her subordinate. Feeling not only unappreciated, but humiliated, this talented woman felt she had no option but to look for a position in another company. Her previous employer lost someone whose loyalty and dedication to the company was unquestioned.

The need to feel appreciated in our job touches deep nerves in all of us. There are very few things we will not do in a situation where we feel valued and appreciated, and very few things we will do where we feel unappreciated.

Expressing appreciation to those who work for and with you does not have to be a major, time-consuming project. One of the simplest, easiest ways is with the praise and appreciation note.

When I first went to work for Disney, I continually heard one particular executive's name mentioned positively by the Disney employees. Bob was evidently held in high esteem by all who worked with him. Intrigued, I made an appointment just to get acquainted. We had a warm meeting, and I was impressed with his friendly, easy manner.

Two days later, I received a hand-written note on Bob's personal stationery wishing me luck in my new position. I was greatly surprised and delighted that a major vice president would take the time to write me a personal note. As I made inquiries with others, I found that this was at the heart of what made Bob so popular and respected in the organization.

Whenever he worked on a major project, Bob sent each person involved a hand-written note of praise and appreciation. These were not sent to only the project coordinators, mind you. They were also sent to the electricians, audio engineers, painters, designers, and secretaries. Bob communicated clearly that there is no such thing as an unimportant job, no matter how big the project. Consequently, he had one of the most highly motivated departments in the organization. People considered it a privilege to work for him. As a result, Bob's own rise up the corporate ladder was meteoric.

Your office morale, as well as your own success, could be greatly helped if you took just ten minutes a day to write a few words of praise or appreciation to an employee. As others around you begin to practice this as well, a real epidemic of appreciation would sweep your company.

When a friend of mine, Julie, started a new job, I suggested that she begin to use the praise and appreciation note. She had just accepted an entry-level position paying $25,000 a year, but had a strong desire to go much higher in the organization. Julie started practicing the note campaign, combining it with a lot of enthusiasm and a well-groomed visual image.

Morale in her area of responsibility began to noticeably improve, and her positive contribution to the team spirit came to the attention of the CEO of the company. Within a year and a half, Julie was offered a position paying $50,000 a year with greatly increased responsibility. Julie had no college education and much less experience in her position than many others in the company. But Julie had learned the startling power of taking just a few minutes every day to write notes of praise and appreciation to her co-workers.

While in Canada working on the Calgary Olympics project, I shared the note idea with a group of managers and asked them to try it by sending notes to two people under them. Al Richards, director of the convention center in Calgary, picked an elderly cleaning lady. She had worked for him for years, was always on time and pleasant, and looked nice. In fact, because she had so many of the qualities of the perfect employee, he realized she was one of the "overlooked people" in his charge because she was never a problem. Al took just two minutes at the end of one day to write her a note, expressing appreciation for several of the specific qualities he had identified in her.

The next morning, the cleaning lady came into his office, clutching the note and with tears in her eyes. "Never in my life," she said, "has anyone ever given me any recognition". She thanked him profusely for taking the time to write the note. Al told me later that he is certain that he is getting as much out of these exchanges as the people receiving the notes. In these "epidemics of appreciation" everyone feels better about themselves.

Again, what is the pay off? Appreciated employees will create customers who feel appreciated. It is a simple, but powerful concept. What do you think would happen if a wave of appreciation swept over your organization? It would directly translate to dollars in the cash drawer.

The Need for Rewards and Recognition

A second cousin to the need for appreciation is the need for recognition. Recognition is appreciation carried into the public arena, praising someone in front of their peers for doing an especially good job. Offering praise in front of others doubles its impact. A driving force behind occupations such as acting, musicians, humorist, professional speakers and preachers is the instant reward for a job well done. It comes in the form of laughter, applause and standing ovations. It is immediate gratification; every human needs it and every human wants it. But who is clapping for the bookkeeper, the secretary, the janitor or the receptionist? Many of these employees must wait a full year for their reward and then it comes in the form of a cost of living raise. Little satisfaction for a year of dedication to the job.

It is a smart company that understands our need for recognition. Rewards need not be complicated or expensive. An unexpected day off, a gift certificate, a bouquet of flowers, tickets to a sporting event or even an office pizza party.

The return to the company in the form of loyalty, job satisfaction, image and prestige is invaluable. Nothing does more for corporate image than employees who are happy and proud of their company.

Many companies outside the real estate industry, where recognition programs have traditionally been strong, have begun "Employee of the Month" or "Salesperson of the Month" programs with great success.

Now let's mention a word that is not often heard in circles of business people. Fun. It is becoming clearer and clearer that fun and laughter are great ways to help people relax, help people feel joy connected to their work. Therefore it enables employees and employers to feel more loyal and less stressed all at the same time. Creating an environment where fun is allowed also promotes creativity.

The Need for Growth and Advancement

A very interesting piece of research was published recently in USA Today under the headline "Why Workers Quit Their Jobs." In a nationwide survey of exiting employees, the consulting firm of Robert Half International found, surprisingly, that money was at the bottom of the list of reasons for quitting. Heading the list, cited by 47 percent of those surveyed, was limited advancement. Another 26 percent gave lack of recognition as the reason they quit. The conclusion is obvious and reinforces the point I have been making.

The key to low turnover, the key to increased motivation, is not primarily meeting monetary needs. The key is meeting emotional needs. Tops among those needs, according to the Robert Half survey, is the need for unlimited advancement opportunities, followed closely by the need for recognition.

Both advancement and recognition fulfill our inner need to feel important, to feel significant. We will even accept less money if we can earn the right to increased responsibility and the recognition that comes with it.

Honda recognizes this drive for advancement. It promotes from within its own ranks, rather than hiring its managers from the outside. As a result, employee turnover is only 2 percent—minuscule compared to the rest of the industry.

When veteran employees are passed over in favor of hiring managers from the outside, morale plummets. Workers feel that no matter how hard they work, it will not make any difference; they will never have the advancement opportunities they desire.

This is not to say there are not hard decisions to be made in determining an employee's suitability for promotion. An employee's sense of opportunity for advancement has more to do with overall corporate philosophy than with individual situations. The point is, companies with an open-ended advancement policy, who look for ways to promote and recognize their people, are rewarded with a highly motivated, very loyal work force, greater productivity, and low employee turnover. That translates directly into financial success for the business.

The Need for Caring

Meet Steve and Bill, two executives who get their respective jobs done, but by radically different styles of management. Steve came straight out of the old school of top-down authoritarianism. A hard-driving, all-business type of manager, he believed the office was no place for personal involvement with his employees. The emotional or human side of his people was never acknowledged. The focus was the project. Steve refused all invitations to social situations, and never recognized any personal events in the lives of his staff. Steve met his deadlines and completed his projects, but he enjoyed almost no loyalty from his staff. His people worked for him, not with him, and the first chance they got, many transferred out.

By contrast, Bill deliberately took interest in the emotional side of his employees. At least once a year, each staff member, regardless of rank, was invited into his office for an informal chat. Bill would move out from behind his desk and sit with the employee at his conversation area. Business was never discussed during these meetings. The only purpose was to relate on a personal level. "How are you? How's the family? Don't I recall hearing about a new boat?" were the kinds of questions Bill asked, listening to the answers with genuine interest. The conversations were friend to friend, not superior to subordinate.

Bill sent sympathy cards, congratulatory cards, and even baby gifts. He personally visited the hospital with a coloring book and crayons for the sick child of an employee. In all these ways, Bill filled the need employees have to feel cared for. He acknowledged that his people were more than units of productivity; they were human beings. His staff responded with the highest levels of loyalty.

William Walton, the former president of Holiday Inns, used to walk through his Memphis headquarters once a year at Christmas time and talk to every employee personally, from vice presidents to janitors. He knew most of them on a first name basis and sought to communicate that he valued each one of them personally.

These are the kinds of efforts that create employee bonding with the company. When employees feel cared about, respected and appreciated, they love their company and represent it with energy and enthusiasm to customers. Employee attitudes are the biggest challenge in the internal image equation. Now with that challenge behind us, we are ready to examine the important role of training in customer relations.

❖ ❖ ❖

Research shows that 68 percent of customers are lost due to rude or indifferent treatment. Another 14 percent are lost due to grievances that are not satisfactorily adjusted. A business may have a great product and technically knowledgeable people, but the key is development of customer-friendly staff. This is where employee appreciation really pays off; they are the ones who will make your customers feel important.

The most successful companies know that specific training in how to relate to customers is important. Without training, employees will simply use their own standards to determine what is appropriate. Disney requires all new employees to attend three days of initial training and regular refresher courses later on. Corning Glass requires all employees to take two weeks of additional training every year. American Express, Motorola, Rubbermaid, and Lands' End dominate their markets by training every employee in every division to focus on the customer.

At American Express, employees are encouraged to figure out how they would want to be treated as card members and trained in specific social skills, like using customers' names. Lands' End trains its telephone operators in the advanced art of helping unseen customers feel important. As one Lands' End operator put it: "Customers expect an awful lot from us, and we have to make each one feel like he is the most important person we talk to today. It's not always easy, but we do it."

In helping Calgary prepare for the Winter Olympics, I carried out a mass training program for everyone in the hospitality industry. The training focused on how to be friendly, helpful, and courteous. Public service videos were developed for corporate training programs. One segment, for example, highlighted taxi drivers, demonstrating to them how to be helpful. It showed a cab driver explaining to a tourist couple, "Now I can take you into town for $17, or you can take the bus for $7."

Specific training in how to put the customer first is absolutely essential to developing a positive internal image. A positive internal image, in turn, brings repeat customers and a solid, long-term business reputation.

When employees are rude or incompetent, the responsibility

rests with the person at the top. Managers reflect the attitudes of the board room, and front-line employees reflect their managers. Everything affecting the image of your business is a legitimate concern.

Several years ago, my husband and I were returning from two years in the West Indies. Anxious to find a new home quickly, we made an appointment with a real estate broker in Newport Beach, California. As I entered the building, I was impressed with the tasteful decor. I was likewise impressed with the manner and professionalism of the broker during our interview. When we finished our interview, the broker called in a nicely groomed agent and suggested she show us several homes.

As we followed the saleswoman to the parking lot, I scanned the parked cars and said to myself, "I hope it's not the yellow car." The yellow car was not only quite small for tall people, it was also in dire need of a wash. Sure enough, we headed straight for the yellow car. As she opened the door, the agent said to my husband, "Don't mind the mess in the back seat. Just push all that clutter over to one side."

Meanwhile, in the front seat, I was brushing cigarette ashes that had overflowed from a sand-bottom ash tray jammed between the front seats and crammed full of butts. By this time, the whole situation was almost humorous until we pulled out of the parking lot and this lady lit a cigarette in a closed car with two non-smokers! Our relationship with this salesperson was over before it had a chance to begin.

Putting the customer first means training your people in the dozens of little courtesies and skills that add up to saying, "We care about you, and we'd really like your business."

External image opens the door of opportunity. It is your internal image that ensures it is not a revolving door.

BUDGETING FOR IMAGE

Everything that we have been discussing does not happen automatically or without some expense. The role of financial planning can not be overemphasized. Without it you may find that the company has all kinds of reasons for not promoting and supporting programs for employee morale. It often takes a major shift in thinking to realize that caring about employees will result in increased customer satisfaction and a healthier profit margin. The paradox is that you begin at the end when you are putting together your financial plan. This means that you must visualize every detail of the image and reputation you desire for your company. I have personally been using the techniques of visualization most of my life and have seldom found it to fail. Visualize the smallest details, from the design of your business cards to the color of your company cars. Visualize your customer service and product quality standards. Visualize your charity giving, and community involvement, and the story that will appear in Fortune and Newsweek. Visualize every aspect of your business that will determine your future reputation. Visualization serves as a blue print for the brain. When the visualization process is complete write every thing down. You have now established your long term image and reputation goals. Once these are established you will have a better idea of your financial needs and will be far less likely to a make a costly mistake of under budgeting. If you truly believe in the power of positive image and the roll it plays in your long term business and personal success do not skimp for necessities only. Budget for image projection without fear. It is not superficial. It is smart.

A successful business man and friend shared with me his history. While still young and broke but with a strong personal belief system he borrowed money to rent an office on expensive Wilshire Blvd in Los Angeles. He surrounded his newly formed production company with the perception of success. The perception quickly became a reality.

If your company is in image trouble, the image has slipped or simply the image is not as positive as you would like it to be, you may need an image coordinator. Companies specializing in the development or improvement of image are competent in analyzing the intangible, internal, and external areas of your organization. This is wise financial planning as large sums of money can easily be wasted on projects that improve the image very little. If you hire an advertizing agency without a total plan your image money could be used totally for advertizing. The same is true for a public relations or interior design firm. Without a coordinated plan the agencies will focus only on their specialty area, which is certainly understandable. Do not put all of your image eggs in one basket.

Each year before budget meetings review the image Masterplan. Reject the temptation to expand at the cost of allowing present standards to slip. The desire for more, greed, often overrides the common sense decision to put your existing facilities in A-1 condition. The Howard Johnson chain made this error with their motor lodges. Once the image is gone, it is costly and difficult to recover.

6

The Emotional Connection
The Essential Ingredient

The primary human emotional need is to feel valued as an individual. We begin life as the center of our universe. Despite the non-stop hard knocks we take from that point on, we stubbornly hold on to the need to feel special, valued, and important.

Following Michael Dukakis's disastrous defeat in the 1988 presidential election, Dukakis's campaign coordinator John Sasso was asked by *Newsweek* for his analysis of why his man lost. Sasso summed it up by saying the issue that defeated Dukakis was not ideology or competence. Rather, he lost because of the lack of "an emotional connection" between himself and the American people. The main lesson he learned from the experience, Sasso said, was that "a presidential candidate can't win without making the emotional link to the voters."

Is it possible that an intelligent, informed electorate, after the most exhaustive campaign in U. S. history, chose the next president not on the basis of competency, but on the basis of an emotional connection with the candidate? It is not what people know but what they feel that makes them act or react.

What happens when your business reaches out to people and makes them feel special? You prosper! Capture your clients' hearts and they will give you their dollars. It is really that simple, but it requires determination and hard work to capture and keep the hearts of your clients to make an emotional connection.

THE MISSING INGREDIENT

The longer I am in business, the more convinced I am that the difference between winning and losing in the image game lies in that one key ability to make an emotional connection. Nordstrom is one of the retailing success stories of the 1980s. Does it carry merchandise so different from other upscale department stores? No. Are its locations that much better than its competition? No. The difference is the attitude of its employees.

It does not matter whether you shop during one of Nordstrom's sales or you pay full price, you receive the same great level of service. Whether you spend fifteen or fifteen hundred dollars, you will be treated with courtesy, respect, and a sincere desire to be of service. Does this happen by accident? No. This attitude starts at the top of the corporate pyramid and is encouraged throughout the organization.

Whether you make a purchase, or not, many Nordstrom sales associates will get your address and, if possible, your phone number. A few days later you will receive a hand-written thank you note. In the coming months you will receive notes about the arrival of new merchandise the sales associate thinks you might like, based upon stated preferences and purchases. This kind of attention from a retail store makes you feel special. Can you think of another retail chain that has inspired license plate frames that read, "I'd Rather Be Shopping At Nordstrom" and "University of Nordstrom?" There is even a noun to describe someone who shops at Nordstrom: a "Nordie."

How does Nordstrom achieve this level of loyalty in the hotly competitive world of retail clothing? By consistently making their customers feel special and appreciated. Can this work in other endeavors as well? It certainly can!

For twelve years I banked with a very large commercial bank. When I opened my account, I was making average money and received average customer service. The bank manager never introduced himself; in fact he never came out of his office. My only memory of this bank manager during the entire twelve years was the sight of him sitting in his office at his desk reading, never taking the time to look up at the activity in the bank.

When I began to speak and work as a consultant, my bank account started to grow. I bought certificates of deposit, made investments, and increased my savings account. I became a frequent visitor to the bank, yet the manager stayed in his office, absorbed by whatever he was reading.

One day, I received a call from a competing bank. David, the district manager, opened the conversation by saying, "Bobbie, we want your business!" That is one of the best opening lines a salesperson can use. He wanted my business. He wanted it so badly that he arranged an appointment for me to meet the bank manager, and a private banker was assigned to manage my account. After twelve years of indifference, the message my ego received was, "You, Bobbie Gee, are important to us." As a follow-up to the appointment, I was sent a large fruit basket and a thank you note. What a great beginning.

Both banks gave quality service. The second bank added the missing ingredient: The Emotional Connection. You might think small banks have more leeway to attract customers. The first bank has over 550 branches in the state of California; the second has over 570 branches in the state. Size has nothing to do with service. If you want to do better than the competition, give better service.

A few years ago I saw the power of this principle while visiting my cousin in northern California. She and her husband suggested we go out to dinner at their favorite restaurant. They both raved about the place, and my expectations steadily built until the evening we arrived. I was disappointed that the restaurant was only average in appearance, I rated the food to be solidly average. Why was this restaurant getting rave reviews from these people?

As soon as we walked through the door, the owner greeted us by name as if he had been waiting for us to arrive. "Good evening, Dr. and Mrs. Brooks. How good to see you! I see you have a guest with you tonight; you get the best table in the house!" This businessman understood the importance of making an emotional connection with his customers. What his restaurant lacked in decor and epicurean delights, he more than made up for with his astute understanding of human nature.

Business goes where it is invited. Business stays where it is well treated. Business grows where it is cultivated.

The Emotional Brain

Many executives reject the idea that emotions play an integral part in the business world. "Don't give me this feelings stuff, Bobbie," I was told by a business executive. "I believe in using my brain to make business decisions and my brain works on logic, not emotions."

Recent studies by two highly respected San Francisco medical researchers have uncovered startling new evidence to prove what some of us have been saying for years that the brain's functions, and especially its decision-making abilities, are governed more by emotions than by logic. Drs. David Sobel and Robert Ornstein, neurologists at the University of California Medical Center, have identified a "command center" within the brain that controls our decisions and functions or talents. Does this command center work primarily on the basis of logic or emotion? Sobel and Ornstein tell us:

> We might hope that a rational and judicious component of the human brain controls and orchestrates this parade of talents. Unfortunately for those who hold such a view, but fortunately for the survival of the organism, the commanding, controlling mental operations system . . . is much more closely linked with emotions and the system of automatic body guards than with conscious thought and reason . . . We have a brain that operates much more with emotions in mind than reason.

The 85/15 Formula for Decision Making

The basis behind the principle of making an emotional connection is the "85/15 Formula." Successful salespeople and business people alike understand this principle very well. The "85/15 Formula" is simple: in general, we make decisions based 85 percent on our feelings and only 15 percent on the cold, hard facts. We may use the facts to help justify a decision we want to make, but we generally make our decisions for emotional reasons.

If it were not for the emotions of the human ego, billions of dollars of image products would not be sold each year. Surveys conducted by car manufacturers document this principle year after year. The American public buys cars primarily on the basis of style and color, those features that more directly touch our emotions, rather than for functional or mechanical reasons. Think of your most prized possessions. How many of them were purchased for strictly logical, as opposed to emotional, reasons.

It is because of this "85/15 Formula" that every successful sales person knows that L.Q. is more important than I.Q. "Likability Quotient" is more important than Intelligence Quotient. In some cases, it is just as important as product knowledge. If someone likes you, they will tend to trust you, and will want to do business with you. I am convinced that most sales people do not need another seminar on "Farming the Suburbs" or "999 Ways to Close." They probably just need a simple course in human relations.

In my consulting work, I occasionally find a business that seems to be doing everything right but is still failing. It has good products, a healthy advertising budget, competent management . . . and a bottom line with chronic anemia. Invariably, my study of such a business will reveal a total neglect of the "85/15 Formula."

I usually find customers are treated in a nonchalant, indifferent manner. The business operates as if the factual or technical side of its product or service is more than enough to maintain customers. That may be enough to initially attract customers, but no business will attain long-term success and a loyal customer base without training its employees to make that crucial "emotional connection" with customers.

THE THREE LEVELS OF EMOTIONAL CONNECTIONS

It is not difficult to learn the art of making an emotional connection. The short-term connection often involves nothing more than taking the initiative to give a sincere compliment or ask a caring question.

Ten years ago, I invited my daughter on one of my speaking trips to New York. It was her first time in the city and she was excited. She had saved a great deal of money for shopping and was anxious to spend it. But as we walked from boutique to boutique along the Avenues, I was amazed at the indifference we encountered from the salespeople. Here we were, two women dying to spend our money, and we rarely heard a simple, "May I help you."

At least that was true until we stepped into Elizabeth Arden's. Immediately, a well-dressed, middle-aged woman walked toward us, smiling. Locking her eyes on my daughter, she said, "What a gorgeous young lady you are!" Then, stepping back and looking at the two of us, she said, "Are you two sisters? You look so much alike. Surely you're not her mother!" Turning to another saleswoman she called out, "Marie, look at these two beauties!" Then she turned back to us and said, "How may I help you?"

This saleswoman was a true professional. I would like to believe her compliments were spontaneous, but even if they were not, I so admired her enthusiasm and skill, I encouraged my daughter to do her spending right there.

If you want a truly powerful business image, one that locks in customers emotionally, there are three levels of emotional power skills you and your employees must master. One involves training employees in how to treat customers with basic politeness and how to avoid the more flagrant types of rudeness. Level Two skills focus on expressing appreciation for customers' business. And the highest skill level has to do with touching the deepest nerve of need in the customer: the need to feel important.

Level One: The Need for Politeness

There are some societies that do an excellent job of training in this crucial area. During my tenure at Disneyland as Image Coordinator over a decade ago, I had an encounter with the politeness of the Japanese people that I will never forget. My job often took me out and about the park on inspection tours. As I walked around, I occasionally noticed a strange phenomenon. Whenever I walked by a group of Japanese tourists, the noise level would go up. I would look around to see what had made them so excited, but I never saw anything special. Then it finally dawned on me. It was me, all six feet of me. Obviously, the Japanese visitors had seldom seen a woman that tall.

One day I was coming out of the Pirates of the Caribbean attraction when I looked up and saw a group of about sixty Japanese businessmen coming toward me, all between sixty and seventy-five years old. The street was narrow there in New Orleans Square, so I would have to pass right through the middle of this group. I thought to myself, "Oh, no. Not today. I just don't feel like being one of the attractions at Disneyland today." But then I thought, "To heck with it. Why not give them a thrill?"

I squared my shoulders, straightened to my full height, put on my brightest smile, and plunged into the middle of the group. Sure enough, as I passed through, the noise level went way up. As I reached the other side, I became curious. I had heard of the legendary politeness of the Japanese, and I wondered if, in my case, they might be tempted to turn around and stare. I took a peek behind me, and what I saw absolutely made my day. Not one man in that entire group had turned around to look at me. But, the entire back row, while continuing to walk straight ahead, had their cameras on their shoulders pointed backwards, clicking furiously! I doubled over with laughter right there in the street. And I was given an example of ingrained politeness I will always remember.

Many managers mistakenly assume their employees know how to treat customers with politeness. In all too many situations the opposite is true: there is a critical epidemic of indifference, and in some cases, outright rudeness, that has gripped American business.

Sometimes a lack of politeness can be corrected with simple instruction, such as telling your employees to never, under any circumstances, leave a customer waiting at the counter in order to answer a potential customer's questions on the phone. Either do both transactions simultaneously if it is nondisruptive or place the caller on hold while completing the transaction with the customer at the counter. It may seem obvious business etiquette to give higher priority to an on-premise money-spending customer than to a phone inquirer. It is not safe, however, to assume that all employees automatically know what is obvious. In most cases, they must be trained in how to be polite.

Sometimes the problem is one of attitude and not so easily solved. Recently, I ordered fifty dollars worth of flowers for a special occasion and asked the florist to have them ready by ten o'clock the next day. The following day an urgent situation arose at the office which demanded my total attention. About eleven o'clock the florist called me. He asked if I was still planning to pick up the flowers and relayed in an irritated tone that he had gone to special trouble to have them ready by ten. When I was finally free from the office, I drove to the florist and picked up the flowers, never to return again.

The florist had forgotten one of the first rules of business etiquette: his purpose is to serve the customer; the customer is not to serve him. Those businesses that know the rules and follow them retain their customers. Those that do not lose their customers to competitors. Your employees need instruction in the art of being polite. In our society, you simply cannot assume that your employees have been taught how to be polite and avoid being rude.

Level Two: The Need to Appreciate

Level Two skills involve expressing appreciation to your customers for their business. Ask yourself how much money you spend on advertising to attract new customers. Now ask yourself how much money you budget for appreciation programs to keep the customers you already have. Also ask yourself who receives most of your attention. Is it the 20 percent of your customers who never seem to pay their bills on time. What about the 80 percent who do pay on time? Are you taking them for granted?

Notes can be a very effective way to express appreciation to your customers. For example, if you are a dentist, try sending a hand-written note to each new patient. Do you sell real estate? Send a note with a bouquet of flowers to your clients who have just moved into the house you sold them.

Do you want to make your clients and customers feel appreciated and valued? Do you want to make them feel important? Send them a short, hand-written note.

Another way to make your customers feel special is to ask their opinion. Stewart (or Stew) Leonard of Norwalk, Connecticut, manages a family-owned food store that began as a dairy in 1921. The average U. S. supermarket carries 16,000 items and grosses around $200,000 a week. By contrast, Mr. Leonard stocks only 740 items and grosses around $1. 5 million per week. How does Mr. Leonard obtain such phenomenal results? He asks his customers what they want, then listens to their answers; he asks, and then listens.

Stew Leonard walks the aisles of his store daily, making himself visible and available for compliments, complaints, and comments. He greets; he chats; he visits; he even hugs. In general, he tries to communicate his appreciation to all his customers. Customers are also invited to participate in bimonthly focus groups to communicate what they like and do not like. Mr. Leonard compliments his customers by listening and responding. They in turn show their appreciation at the cash register to the tune of $80 million a year.

Contrast the Stew Leonard experience with what we have come to expect from our local supermarkets. Please note, this is not an isolated case of just one market; the disease I describe is of epidemic proportions. It is the end of your day. You are tired. All you want to do is get home, but you must stop by the market to pick up a few items. You get the items, get in the express line, and wait. Four registers are not being used, and you are waiting. It doesn't matter whether you have a few items or a whole basket load; you are going to wait. Does it sound as if this market wants your business? It gets better.

Once you reach the cashier, you have the opportunity to listen to the cashier and bagger carry on a conversation that covers a variety of personal topics. Are you addressed at all? Is there a hello? A thank you?

These markets spend millions of dollars in advertising to get you in the door. How much do they spend on training their employees to treat the customer with common courtesy and appreciation? If they would just spend a little on employee training in ways to make the emotional connection these markets would see a tremendous rise in their bottom line. Stew Leonard has proven that time and time again.

Level Three: The Need to Feel Important

All your customers and potential customers have a variety of unmet emotional needs: a need for respect, a need for appreciation, a need to feel good about themselves. Beyond these is the number-one human emotional need: the need to feel important. That need runs so deep in each one of us that we can base our whole lives around a search for it or be scarred by its absence.

Following a seminar of mine about the power of words to touch others emotionally, an elderly lady approached me and asked if we could speak for a few minutes. What she had to tell me brought home the true power we all have to influence people by what we say and do.

She began, "My husband and I are living examples of what you've told us about the power of words, but in two very different ways. When I was fifteen years old and walking out the front door on my first date, my father looked at me and said, 'Who could ever love you?' I am sixty-five years old and have never forgotten those words.

"But my husband has a different story to tell," she continued. "He's seventy years old and was raised an orphan. He never received the attention or praise he so desired as a child. At age seventeen, he was walking off the football field when his coach stopped him, put his arms around my husband's shoulders and said, 'Son, that is the best football game I have ever seen anyone play.' "

With a glint of pride in her eye, the woman concluded, "My husband built the rest of his life around that one sentence. He traces all the major achievements of his life back to that day when his coach told him he was somebody special."

The highest skill level in customer relations is the ability to touch that inner need to feel important. This is where the emotional connection takes place and loyal customers are created. Despite the rarity of this skill, it is not difficult to practice and master.

The most obvious thing you can do is compliment your customers on their appearance. "That is a beautiful dress." "What a handsome tie." "That is a beautiful ring." It can go on and on, but remember that it is important to be sincere about what you are saying.

If you know your customers a little better, ask them about their families, their recent vacations, or wish them a happy birthday. What I am saying is that you should get a little more personal in what you say to make your client or customer feel important. When you get right down to it, your customers are of great importance to you. If they do not buy your product or service, you do not make money. It is that simple.

What happens if your customers also provide a service for you? They could be your dentist, your lawyer, your gardener, pool cleaner, or child's teacher. What would happen if you made them feel important? What would happen if you took a few extra moments to recognize them as people as well as the job they are doing for you? They would feel much better about themselves and about you; they would want to do a better job.

How can you train your employees to meet your customers' need to feel important? In the first few moments of contact with a prospective customer, employees should be trained to forget about the product and concentrate totally on the individual. Let us say you own a real estate agency and a client has made an appointment with one of your associates to view houses next week. Your associate has been trained to ask questions during the initial telephone interview, and learns that your client is a long-haul truck driver for a big freight company. In the five days before the appointment, your associate finds out a little bit about his new client's company; how big it is, the kind of freight it carries, just general things.

On the appointment day, the sales associate knows to delay selling real estate for a few minutes so that he can relate to his client's life and lifestyle. He may say something like: "I don't know how you truckers do it. That's one tough job. But I'm sure glad you do. Most people have no idea the products they'd be without if it weren't for you truckers." The associate then relates his acquired knowledge of his client's company. In 30 seconds to a minute your associate has complimented your client, put him at ease and made him feel important.

Do you understand the power what you say can have over people? You can choose to build up others, to make them feel important. What will happen if you begin to do this? You will guarantee yourself a loyal customer base.

A SIGN OF SUCCESS

M. Y. MY. "My" is a very significant word in achieving success. In the competitive world of business, these two letters spell the difference between success and failure. You will know you are achieving success by making an emotional connection when you hear your customers use the word "my."

The power of that word struck home several years ago when my daughter called me full of excitement. "Mom, guess what? I've decided to buy a house! It's so much fun looking at homes. And, Mom, my real estate agent is so nice!" It struck me that my daughter had used "my" to describe a real estate agent she had just met.

"My lawyer . . . "

"My jeweler . . . "

"My mechanic . . . "

"My florist . . . "

"My . . . "

Those are the magic phrases that tell you, you are successful. You are successful not just in terms of business, but in reaching out to people to make an emotional connection. You can give outstanding service to your clients and still remain "the . . . ", but if you want to become "my . . ." you must touch their hearts.

When clients refer to you in terms of ownership they are emotionally hooked. They are locked into your business. They create a loyal customer base from which you can go on to the heights of success. It also becomes extremely difficult for a competitor to lure your clients away. When your clients cannot be lured away, you are beginning to assure yourself of long-term success.

Even if you have a monopoly on selling one particular item in an area, you cannot take your clients for granted. Number one, you may not always have that monopoly; number two, your clients will make more purchases.

Jimmy owns a small chain of restaurants. He started out by selling sandwiches at lunch time from a little place off the beaten path. He did not sell very many sandwiches at first, but he stuck it out, learned from his mistakes, and grew.

In the beginning, he bought his supplies from two sources. One of the salespeople spent time with Jimmy to give him guidance. He gave him recipes, suggested menu changes, and even suggested advertising techniques. The other salesperson usually phoned because he did not have enough time to personally attend to such a small account.

Jimmy grew. At first, it was just an increase in sales. Then he grew to another location, then several locations. Who do you think was selling him all his supplies? It was the salesman who took the time to see and talk with Jimmy every week. Jimmy had made an emotional commitment to the first salesman. He could have bought his supplies elsewhere, and even for less money, but he just could not do that to his friend, the salesman.

Was it good business for this salesman to invest time in such a small account? Did it pay off to treat Jimmy as though he had a chain of restaurants? Was it worth it to make Jimmy feel important? Yes, yes, and yes.

Jimmy, for his part, also had a knack for making his customers feel important. Not only did he know them by name, all his employees knew most of their customers by name and what they normally had to eat. He also listened to customers' comments and often made special sandwiches for customers. Did this have anything to do with his success? Of course, it did.

The competition is fierce in the restaurant industry, especially in fast-food service. Jimmy knew that any one of his customers could go to the local McDonalds or other fast-food establishment for lunch, but he could not allow that to happen if he were going to be a success. What did he do? He made an emotional bond between himself and his customers. He made them feel important every time they stepped into his restaurant. He became "my lunch place" for a lot of people.

Remember that a business may be the greatest looking, the best maintained, the most beautifully decorated, and the most skillfully advertised of its kind in town. But it will always remain *the* cleaners or *the* video store until its employees are taught how to touch their customers emotionally by making them feel special.

Several years ago I placed a Christmas order for three beautiful trays from Gumps, the image-conscious gift store in San Francisco. When I received my order, I saw that I had been sent one large tray instead of the three small trays I had ordered. I called Mrs. Willis in Gumps Customer Service Department and explained the mistake. Very apologetic, Mrs. Willis assured me she would take care of everything. Two weeks later my order still had not arrived and Christmas was imminent. I called once again and Mrs. Willis was embarrassed. Shortly I received my correct order. I called Mrs. Willis to tell her I still had the large tray I had not ordered, and I would be happy to have it charged to my credit card as well. Much to my surprise, Mrs. Willis said, "Keep it, and consider it Gumps present to you and our apology for the trouble we've caused you."

Do you think that treatment developed customer loyalty in me? You better believe it! Every year I travel from my home in southern California to San Francisco in order to do my Christmas shopping at my Gumps.

My loyalty did not happen by accident. It was obvious to me that Gumps had done at least two important things to create Mrs. Willis's response: it had a clearly defined set of company policies and procedures to cover circumstances like mine, and it thoroughly trained Mrs. Willis to handle those circumstances, including giving her the authority to make necessary decisions on the spot. That is a good example of how a company can train its employees to give a level of service such that even mistakes can ultimately produce customer loyalty.

THE EMPLOYEE CONNECTION

Making an emotional connection works not only with clients and customers; it is a smart and effective way to treat your employees. If you want to move beyond the management skills of "Management 101", you must practice with your employees the three skill levels we have just examined.

If you, as a manager or owner, treat your employees with politeness and courtesy, they will treat your customers in the same fashion. Why? Because your employees feel good about themselves, you, and the job they are doing. A little praise will go a long way.

However, if you mistreat your employees by criticizing them in front of others, by demeaning the job they are doing, or by displaying uncontrolled anger, they will get the idea it is okay to act that way and begin to treat your customers and clients in the same fashion. They will not respect you or your firm, and your clients will come to know this from the way they are treated.

Some managers and owners have the mistaken idea that

liberal amounts of praise will lead employees to overestimate their monetary worth. Wrong. Most people value recognition even more highly than money. Once again, the need to feel important is the greatest human emotional need. Praise is not usually viewed by employees as a means toward more money. Praise is prized as an end in itself. Recognition for a job well done is a motivator in and of itself.

During an annual real estate rally in Texas, one employee was walking off with award after award and beaming each time she walked across the stage. Afterward, I asked the broker about this superstar.

"Has she spent quite a few years building her business?"

"No, she's only been in real estate a short time."

"Well, what's her secret?" I asked.

He looked toward the beaming salesperson and said, "Ann's really not that motivated by money. What she has is a deep need to be recognized, praised, and appreciated. So I've structured an awards program to meet that need." A slight smile began to spread across his face as he said, "It's working, isn't it?"

Ann gets recognized for producing sales, which makes her feel important. More sales means more money for the broker. He has tapped into the source of Ann's motivation to be recognized for her contribution to the benefit of both. That is good business sense.

A CAUTIONARY NOTE

Is all this talk about touching people emotionally mere manipulation? Obviously, as with any powerful skill, emotional connection can be abused, but it does not have to be. At its best it involves sensing what someone really wants, what emotional need a client or employee would like to have filled, and seeking to meet it in the process of providing your service or product.

Many years ago Joseph Day, the greatest real estate salesperson of his time in New York City, was contacted by Robert Gray, the president of the U. S. Steel Corporation. Since its inception,

U. S. Steel had leased offices in the Empire State Building. Now, Mr. Gray explained, the time had come for U. S. Steel to buy a building of its own. Day did his research on buildings throughout the city, but he could not get away from a growing conviction that the most suitable building for U. S. Steel to purchase was the very building they were now leasing—the Empire State Building.

On the day of the presentation, the president of U. S. Steel opened the conversation with disappointing news. "I'm afraid, Mr. Day, that we have already found a building that appears to suit our needs." Day was crushed, but he began to ask Mr. Gray a series of questions to draw out what it was he really wanted. They talked for a while, then Day quietly said, "May I ask, sir, where U. S. Steel was formed?"

"Why, right here in this very building," replied Mr. Gray, his eyes twinkling.

"And where was your first office?"

"The same, right here."

The salesman deliberately sat quietly and let the memories grow in his client's mind.

Finally Mr. Gray spoke up. "My junior officers want a new building, but this is our home. We were born here, and I love this building. This is the one we should buy."

Within half an hour a five-million-dollar deal was closed. Joseph Day clearly understood the power of emotions, of finding the emotional needs of a potential customer, then seeking to meet those in the process of doing business.

7

Maintaining Your Image

In 1984 I received a call from a committee of Calgary Canada business leaders. Calgary had been chosen as the host city for the 1988 Winter Olympic games and they were faced with two basic issues. One was the negative attitudes and the general lack of enthusiasm by the citizens of Calgary. The second was what image to project during the games.

The first problem was easy to understand because the oil boom had turned into the oil bust. Empty, boarded up houses were prevalent throughout the city as many oil company employees had moved on and business revenues had taken a serious down turn.

The second problem was complicated by the existence of opposite opinions on how to project the cities image to the world during the games. One group wanted an up scale sophisticated image befitting a town known for oil production. The other group preferred to stay with the western image they had as host of the annual Calgary Stampede.

My first task was to help them define a city philosophy. We decided on "Calgary . . . We Treat People Special." The philosophy once defined made the mission simple. Treat every guest to the city in an enthusiastic friendly manner. The goal was to have citizens so exceptional the media would become enthusiastic about the people of Calgary. My task was a little harder, how do you instill six hundred thousand people with the vision and desire to act according to the plan. I explained to the committee the principle of "What goes around comes around." If you want the citizens to treat the tourist in a special way, treat the citizen in the same manner. After a presentation to a negative city press they began to understand the long term rewards of becoming more positive. Tourists buy newspapers and merchandise from your advertisers, I suggested, then they caught the vision.

Two years before the games a television station produced short vignettes with a theme song showing the helpful friendly citizen of Calgary helping and enjoying the Olympic Games guest. Video training classes promoting the philosophy and pride in Calgary were presented to large corporations throughout the city.

The people caught the vision and during the games Calgary and its citizens received positive press coverage.

Now what approach should we take to the second problem, a sophisticated image or do we continue with the western theme? I was quick to remind the committee that it was the western image that made Calgary different than hundreds of other North American cities all desperate to attract tourism dollars. I suggested that the image be promoted during the games and Mayor Klien agreed. Always remember that it is your positive difference that sets you apart from the competition. The program was such a success Calgary's convention center has enjoyed a full calendar since the games.

THE REPUTATION EQUATION / I + R = P

It is a simple equation. Image plus Reputation equals Profits. It may be simple and it may take real effort to create it but a positive reputation can be a pretty fragile thing. The Bhopal tragedy, even though it was just one incident, can severely damage the reputation of a company like Union Carbide overnight. One accusation and the reputation of a televangelist that took years to create can be severely tarnished. Image, at its root, is basically a perception, and perceptions are very much subject to change.

Just as much care should go into preserving and protecting a successful image as went into crafting it in the first place. When that is done, companies can survive even unforeseen tragedies with their image intact: witness Tylenol after its cyanide scare or McDonalds after the San Ysidro mass shooting.

One of the occupational hazards of success is carelessness and a certain irrational sense of invulnerability, such as what we saw demonstrated by Richard Nixon in his last years in office. The harsh reality is, none of us is beyond the reach of image backlash if we break the rules.

The Two Commandments

There are a host of rules that pertain to the initial development of a successful business image. Those rules cover everything from your advertized image to the intangibles of how you treat people. But there are only two inviolable rules governing the preservation of a successful business image.

(1) Remain true to your foundation; it is responsible for the success you are now enjoying.
(2) Never sacrifice long-term image for short-term profit.

Put another way, your two main enemies in maintaining positive long-term image and reputation are **inconsistency** and **greed**.

The breaking of an image , even if only temporarily, can come with one shocking and unforeseen event, such as the Alaskan oil spill from the Exxon Valdez. But more often the breaking of an image is more subtle. It is a series of long-term events so clouded under a veil of profitability few executives see it coming.

It is much like the drips of water on a granite rock. The rock is so strong no one pays attention to the drips. Then one day the rock splits. I have been asked to repair a broken or tarnished image after years of neglect and molestation, after years of an image being taken for granted. In some cases the damage was so severe that nothing less than a name change would work; sometimes not even that will bring life to an unhealthy company.

It is surprising how few companies put themselves through image analysis when considering a new product or action.

In his book *The IBM Way,* former IBM vice president Buck Rodgers says that an organization's only sacred cow is its principles. He quotes Tom Watson, Jr., son of IBM's founder, as saying: "For any organization to survive and achieve success, there must be a sound set of principles on which it bases all of its policies and actions. But more important is its faithful adherence to those principles."

Many things about a company may change. Product lines may change. IBM, for instance, was originally in the butcher scale business. Aerospace firm Rockwell International first manufactured parking and taxi meters. Even names of companies may change, like International Harvester's transformation into Navistar International. But the bedrock philosophy of the company, its unique mission statement and standards, must never change, or image disintegration is inevitable. Consistent adherence to its foundation can lead a company to greatness.

Greed is just as dangerous a pitfall to long-term image. Greed is the common denominator in the broken images of the savings and loan industry, the Wall Street insider trading scandals, and the defense contractor abuses.

Many people thought Donald Trump had it all, a beautiful wife, family, fame and fortune, but it was not enough. Doctors were doing well before they abused the Medicare system so the government restricted their fees. Greed had set in and unnecessary tests and procedures were routinely ordered on unsuspecting patients until the government said, "Enough!" Reader's Digest put a husband and wife in an old but mechanically perfect car and sent them out to travel the nation's highways. Their assignment was to test the honesty of auto mechanics. It is a sad but true statement that the mechanics failed this test miserably. The greed of many destroyed the image of the honest.

Stories of personal greed could easily fill volumes. Corporate greed, on the other hand, is harder to identify. It often hides behind the guise of good management practices and profit and loss statements.

When every decision is based strictly on the profit and loss statement, trouble lies ahead. The question "Is this decision wise for my company's economic health?" is obvious, but do not stop there. Expand the question. "How will this affect my reputation and image in the eyes of the public and business community?" It is very easy to say yes to the bottom line if you think only about the immediate profitability of your company. If you think about your future you must look beyond immediate profits and consider how a decision will affect your reputation and image.

The Presence of Tomorrow

Look beyond today, into tomorrow, whenever you are facing any decision. In the brewing industry, stories are still told of how once-powerful Schlitz switched to a cheaper brewing process in the early 1970s in an attempt to increase profits and the net result was that it ultimately destroyed its brand image. Whether the story is true or not is not the point, the effect on the image at that time was unmistakable.

While in New Zealand, I was asked to spend a day consulting with the owner of the only amusement park in Auckland. I was looking forward to seeing the park and especially one new ride that had been the subject of an extensive advertising campaign. The day of the tour came, and my guide pointed out the new attraction. I could hardly believe my eyes. Open dirt and unfinished landscaping surrounded a half-completed facade. What made it worse was the long line queued up in front. The ride was in operation, without a completed exterior.

"How long has this ride been open?" I asked my guide.

"About a month," he said. "The board of directors made a decision to open the ride as soon as it was operable so as not to miss any revenues."

Never have I seen a better example of sacrificing long-term image for short-term profits. The company had spent thousands of dollars to advertise its new attraction, then ruined that all-important first impression for the sake of a few short-term dollars. That is roughly equivalent to a major automaker announcing a new model car with a major ad campaign, only to have the public arrive at the showrooms to find the cars with half-completed chassis. This kind of rush for profits is often the beginning of the end of a business image.

Heroes or Villains?

The image and reputation of individual business leaders is just as vulnerable to the pitfalls of inconsistency and greed. Yesterday's heroes can easily become today's villains if the public perceives them to be breaking the rules. In 1986, Lee Iacocca seemed to be a living legend. He brought Chrysler back from the brink of bankruptcy and was a symbol of the "can do" American fighting spirit. His gesture of taking a salary of only one dollar a year endeared him to thousands of Chrysler union workers and others. He was even prominently mentioned as a possible candidate for president of the United States.

Then came Iacocca's series of decisions to close a number of plants and lay off thousands of workers in order to cut costs, while at the same time accepting a salary of more than $18 million. During this period, Iacocca became the highest paid executive in America, and Chrysler workers began wearing buttons saying, "Iacocca is a liar." On top of that came federal charges of odometer tampering by company executives who were driving newly built cars before they were sold to the public. Overnight, jokes began circulating around the country. "Would you buy a used car from Lee Iacocca?" Because Iacocca had implemented business practices that were inconsistent with the principles of the company, his own image was tarnished. He had fallen into the first pitfall of inconsistency.

Right or wrong, the public perceived Iacocca to have fallen into the second pitfall of greed as well. Whether he had earned his large salary or not is not the issue. The point is that a leader earns the respect of those he leads by avoiding an image of profiting at their expense. No company and no business leader can continue for long to be held in esteem by the public once the employees have become disillusioned.

Perhaps no major corporate executive in America today is a

clearer example of the disintegration of an image from the inside out than Frank Lorenzo. The head of Texas Air had become the executive we most loved to hate, largely because his own employees were so openly hostile toward him.

Early admiration for Lorenzo's talent in turning a small Texas airline into one of the major U. S. contenders was shattered during his brutal 1983 union-busting actions with newly acquired Continental. He declared Continental bankrupt, then immediately reopened it as a non-union carrier and cut employees' salaries in half.

Lorenzo's confrontational style of management earned him the unending enmity of his workers. His battered internal image seems to have permanently tarred his external image with the public. Fortune, for instance, consistently ranked Texas Air as one of the least admired companies in America. In my travels, I heard both Continental pilots and flight attendants openly voice bitter criticism of their boss. No executive, no matter how talented or determined, can maintain a positive business reputation with that level of discontent among employees.

Lorenzo's harsh treatment of his employees marked him in the public's eyes as a man who consistently choose profit over people. He so flagrantly violated the second image rule of never sacrificing long-term image for short-term profit, that it appeared to those of us on the outside that Lorenzo had no concern whatsoever for a positive business image.

Leona Helmsley is a perfect example of image backlash. The public image of caring, the image she tried so hard to create through her advertising, and her internal image, the one known by her employees and creditors, were reported by the media as contradictory. The pretense of caring and the reality of callousness brought her to her knees. Leona Helmsley did not seem to respect the intelligence of her fellow human beings. Did she truly believe the public would not accept the media stories documenting her treatment of employees and creditors? The superficial image of perfection was completely overshadowed by her personal reputation of being destructive and abrasive. If image and reality do not walk hand-in-hand, the profits from the image will soon disappear. From what I read and heard it seems accurate to say that Leona Helmsley sacrificed long-term image and reputation for short-term profits and, like many others, it caught up with her.

Image Backlash

Both Frank Lorenzo and Leona Helmsley are more obvious examples of the disintegration of a personal business image. These are two people who, seemingly through greed, have managed to give the impression through the media that they mismanaged companies and misled the public; they are not what their advertising agencies and public relations people wanted us to believe. Can this happen to an American institution known and respected worldwide?

At first glance, The Walt Disney Company does not seem to be an obvious candidate of image backlash. For more than thirty years, the Disney name has enjoyed the kind of worldwide acclaim that puts it in a category by itself. Few other companies come close to the level of adulation reserved for the Magic Kingdom. In addition, under the current leadership Disney's profitability is at an all-time high.

Unknown to most outside the organization, cracks have begun to appear in both its internal and external image. Disney has begun to implement policies that violate both primary image rules. From my experience with hundreds of companies around the world, what we are presently witnessing, despite its current profitability, is what I believe will be seen as policies and attitudes that will one day negatively affect the Disney image.

For several years now, employees at Disneyland and Walt Disney World have known there is increasing unhappiness in the happiest place on earth. In talking with various employees I hear of management styles which seem more rigid and authoritarian. One highly placed employee calls it "management by coercion."

Many employees also feel the "new Disney" has moved from a focus on people to a focus on profits. The employee discount on entrance fees was recently reduced to a minimum. By contrast,

Universal Studios employees get a 50 percent discount on tickets to Disneyland as part of their employee benefits.

During a period when Disney's profitability is at an all-time high, and the CEO was becoming one of the highest paid executives in America, Disney employees have had their wages kept to a minimum. My impression is that just like with Chrysler and Continental, the Disney workers have become convinced their leaders have stepped over the line into an obsession with money.

"The feeling is gone," one veteran employee told me recently. "There's no longer a caring feeling from management. They're basically just interested in the money now." Disillusionment is so strong among employees at Walt Disney World in Orlando that turnover has reached epidemic proportions. Disney officials are hiring hundreds of new employees per month just to replace the losses. Support groups for ex-Disney employees have sprung up around the Orlando area to help individuals cope with their feelings of resentment. These former employees bought the Disney dream, only to find a different reality. As one bumper sticker seen on cars in that city plaintively asks, "Is there life after Disney?"

Without fail, in my study of successful corporations across the country, when the internal image goes and the enthusiasm and morale of the employees go, the image in the public's eyes will begin to unravel soon after.

Obviously, the goal for every business is to make a profit. But when long-term image is sacrificed for short-term profit, the future success of a company is endangered. The CEO of Disney has, indeed, increased the profits of the company to more than $500 million a year and is being hailed throughout the industry as a miracle worker. But there has been a price for those profits.

One of the new key strategies has been to merchandise the Disney mystique more aggressively than ever before. This has included the establishment of non-tourist Disney retail stores selling every imaginable version of Mickey and friends in malls and shopping centers across the country. Short-term revenues have poured in from these stores, but my own sense is that this

could possibly be at the cost of overexposure of Disney memora-
bilia. As one savvy Disney executive confided to me, "In my
opinion. there's too much mouse out there." The mass marketing of an image is a double-edged sword that can ultimately
cause the loss of its unique appeal.

Even more startling, the management opened the doors of
Disney University to outside organizations for a fee. Other companies can study Disney's secrets and can also have their costumes and uniforms made by Disney seamstresses.

The key to achieving success over your competitors in today's
aggressive business climate is to maximize your unique difference as a company. When you deliberately allow other companies to copy your uniqueness for a fee, you may win in the short
run, but you are almost guaranteed to lose in the long run.

Another of the profits-over-people changes from management has been to allow unlimited numbers of guests into the
parks. Previously, the parks would be closed when attendance
reached a "maximum occupancy" level that allowed the crowds
to feel comfortable. Now, for the sake of increased gate revenue,
guests wait in longer lines than ever before. If the average summer wait at an attraction like Space Mountain is now an hour
and a half, will it soon be two hours or two and a half hours?
How much does the public put up with before a company's
image is seriously damaged?

Probably the most controversial change brought about in recent years has been Disney's production of R-rated movies
through its Touchstone Pictures division. This division has had
such success at the box office, in fact, that a similar studio
named Hollywood Pictures has been launched under the Disney
umbrella.

In my opinion, Disney has once again sacrificed long-term
image for short-term profit. Walt Disney's long-standing motto
was "The finest in family entertainment." That was the guiding
philosophy, the corporate uniqueness that put Disney in a class
all its own and brought the company worldwide acclaim. Faithful adherence to the principles upon which a company was

founded makes the difference between continuing on in greatness or slipping back into the middle of the pack.

Management, of course, once claimed that no one knew that Touchstone and Hollywood Pictures were Disney productions. That is clearly absurd, because Touchstone stars regularly appear on the streets of Walt Disney World for promotional events.

It was not necessary to sacrifice the Disney image to ensure profitability. Designer Ralph Lauren was faced with a similar set of choices for his exclusive Polo/Lauren line of clothes. He was encouraged to increase his licensing revenues by expanding his lines to include less expensive items. He and his managers were told they could expand their business by $100 million a year by offering less expensive shoes, watches, and even a line of downscale underwear. But Lauren knew that such a move, even if it was profitable in the short run, would cheapen and ultimately kill his carefully cultivated image.

Once an image is destroyed, it is almost impossible to resurrect. Only time will tell whether the diminishing of employee morale, combined with the mass merchandising of the Disney mystique, will affect the vaunted Disney image. But the cracks in the facade are getting wider, and for my money, the downward spiral in the public's mind has already begun.

THE TARNISHED IMAGE

How does the once positive image of a company become tarnished? Is it like fine silver? Will it corrode when left in the open air? Is it a conscious decision to flaunt the public's opinion? Is it a one time sudden crisis that breaks an image?

It is usually not just one thing that "goes wrong" for a company. It is a series of decisions that lead a company down the path to a negative image. Most companies are strong enough to take a lot of punches to the midsection; however they can only take so much before they are down for the count.

What can go wrong? I have identified at least ten ways in which a company can lose the public's faith. Take a look at the list. Is your company doing any of them? If so, take corrective action NOW.

1. Undefined principles. Everyone thinks they have principles, but do you really? Do you shave the corner off of a deal, thinking that nobody will ever find out. If the answer is yes, you may think you have principles, but they are clearly undefined and at the mercy of the moment.

2. Lack of commitment to existing principles. You have principles, but do you act in accordance with them? Do you pad your expense account? Will you accept an expensive but inappropriate gift? If yes, your principles are once again at the mercy of the moment; they come and go depending on how profitable it would be to have them or not.

3. Shoddy visual standards. Are the weeds pulled? Does your building need painting? Is your receptionist/greeter clean and neat in appearance? Do your employees know what they should wear? Are you reflecting what you want from everyone in your organization regarding outward appearance? Remember, first impressions are lasting impressions. I know it sounds trite, but it is true.

4. Employee disloyalty and dissatisfaction. If your employees are not loyal to your business and begin to express their dissatisfaction, you will begin to lose whatever image you have gained within your community.

5. Exaggerated, unrealistic advertising. Is your advertising honest? Do you stretch the truth about your product? Are you a modern snake oil salesperson that sells a cure-all for whatever ails your customer? Believe me, the customer will turn to bite you and you will have sacrificed short-term profits for long-term positive image.

If you allow an advertising agency total freedom to develop an advertising slogan that cannot be backed up with 100 percent reality, you will create a serious credibility gap that will become an image killer.

6. Negative press. This is for those of you that have an image death wish. This really shows the power of the press. Even if an untrue story is printed, the seeds of doubt are planted in the minds of your customers and the public. The tendency of the public is to always believe the worst, so they will swallow a negative story hook, line, and sinker because they want the mighty to fall.

7. Inferior customer relations. This method will take a little longer to destroy your company than receiving negative press, but it is far more effective because it comes from the mouth of the consumer. If you want to be successful, you must treat your customers as if they were the greatest advertising agency in the world, which they are. Remember, every time one of your customers has a negative experience, twenty people find out. That is twenty future customers.

8. Inferior product quality. Enough said?

9. Greed. This is the number one killer of businesses and business people. Warnings should be given to all graduates of business schools upon graduation. One of the serious occupational hazards of success is carelessness. A certain irrational sense of invulnerability overtakes people's rational thinking. No one is beyond the reach of image destruction if greed takes hold.

10. Indifference. How much money do you spend to attract new customers? How much do you spend to keep the ones you already have? Have you ever had a customer appreciation day? If you do not care about the people who now use your service or buy your goods, your eventual ruin is assured. You may have a great product the public is lining up to buy, but unless your service and commitment is at least as great as your product the public will begin to find a substitute. The customer is a fickle animal that really deserves courting.

Have you recognized yourself or your actions in the preceding list? If you have, you will find that you are on the road to image destruction. The road may be long, but it becomes increasingly steep and slippery and difficult to navigate.

8

Lifestyle and Likability

Lifestyle image is other people's perception of your personal life, relationships, home life, social calendar, integrity, dignity, conduct—of your personal standards, your character. Lifestyle image can be the sole determining factor between two equally qualified candidates for an all-important career promotion.

I was on a cross-country flight when I became fascinated with a conversation between two older and distinguished gentlemen seated behind me. I listened carefully as they determined which man they would finally select to become president and CEO of a large company. For a few hours they discussed the pros and cons of the two candidates.

The leadership abilities of the two men in question were discussed at length. The conclusion was that the two men were equally qualified. The discussion then focused on lifestyle. I was fascinated as I listened to the debate; the final decision was based on the men's wives. "I have met John's wife a number of times, and I just don't think she has the appearance, social skills, or knowledge to carry off the entertaining that goes along with this position." This decision was final.

I had a similar experience with an acquaintance who was president of a large fishing fleet. Instead of a CEO position being discussed, he and his associate were discussing the vacant captaincy of a ship. Again, the decision was based upon the person's perceived character and lifestyle.

Corporations may not discriminate in terms of color, creed, or religion, but they do discriminate. Do the prospective executives play golf? Do they belong to the "right" club? Know the "right" people? In the case of politicians and those being considered for high corporate positions, do they have "marketable" spouses? Nancy Reagan was perceived as pretentious and extravagant so Barbara Bush was a pleasant change. Lifestyle image has become equal to intelligence for political candidates.

I suggest you structure your lifestyle image around the same elements that guide a successful business: personal philosophy, long-term goals, principles, and standards. Your philosophy will provide a foundation for your decisions. Long-term goals will give you a direction. Commitment to your principles will secure your reputation of integrity, and your standards will set you apart.

Respect—what it is or how a leader earns it is not taught at business schools. Yet respect is the soul of reputation. What more could we desire than to end our career with admiration and respect from our peers, friends, and family? The kind of respect I am referring to has little to do with financial acumen or leadership ability. Respect is not for sale. No public relations firm on earth can buy a person respect.

Personal respect means to be worthy of esteem. Americans are desperately in need of heroes, individuals we can respect and hold in high esteem. In the forties and fifties the media protected the lifestyles of public figures. In the past couple of decades, however, private lifestyles were not only exposed, they were exploited. The media was saying, in essence, "No more!"

The eighties will be remembered for many things, but one of the most significant will be that it was the decade we regained a conscious concern for personal conduct. In the sixties and early seventies we were so open-minded our brains almost fell out. But, as it always does, the pendulum swings back. In one short weekend, the man who would be president lost his image and the presidency in a Washington condominium. Images of the rich and famous, and not so famous, are no longer protected; they are exposed.

In 1984, while on my first and only speaking tour with the famous author of *The Power of Positive Thinking*, Dr. Norman

Vincent Peale, I was jolted into the realization of the lengths to which some people go to protect their image and reputation. During a picture-taking session I was seated next to Dr. Peale, and I unconsciously placed my hand on his arm. The session was stopped abruptly. Why? Because I, as a female, was touching Dr. Peale. I thought the aides were being ridiculous, but on thinking about what a scandal sheet could make of that innocent picture, I understood.

Famous people such as Dr. Billy Graham and Dr. Peale have more to lose than the "average" celebrity. The fact that Dr. Peale was forty-five years my senior made no difference. There has never been a hint of scandal surrounding these famous men, and in today's world that is really a record. Why is that? They jealously guard their images, and do absolutely nothing to tarnish them.

The world will no longer look the other way, pretending not to see and pretending that "personal peccadilloes" are okay. The news media will dig and probe until the truth about a person is revealed. The old-fashioned ethics of morality are in style once again. Maybe you feel the old-fashioned principles only apply to those in the limelight, but who knows when the light will turn in your direction? When it does, you have to be ready.

Lifestyle and the Bottom Line

Lifestyle image not only affects your career, your advancement opportunity, and reputation; it could drastically affect your bank balance. Personal fortunes are made by public figures due in part to perceived image. American Express, in looking for new celebrity faces for its advertising, only considers individuals with squeaky clean images. When they find one, they are willing to pay a king's ransom.

The largest corporate sponsorship in music history up to 1991 occurred between Michael Jackson and PepsiCo. You can bet Michael Jackson's lifestyle was of utmost consideration for PepsiCo. Strange rumors had hit the tabloids concerning Jackson's fascination with and attempt to purchase the remains of John Merrick, the "Elephant Man," and those of an Egyptian mummy. Were Michael's eccentricities a problem, or did they add to the public's fascination with his personality? After much deliberation, Michael was seen as a safe investment by PepsiCo. While his lifestyle may seem somewhat out of the ordinary, it is also seen as very clean. He does not use alcohol or drugs, and he has surrounded himself with the image of bodily perfection, inside and out.

If Michael Jackson could influence the way young people dressed and danced, just maybe he could influence what they chose to drink. Legends surrounding him and his image may shift and change, but for now, Michael is not only a musical icon, he represents the American dream. PepsiCo was quite willing to line the pockets of the most successful pop star ever with millions of dollars due to the selling power of his image.

Nadia Comaneci, the Olympic Gold Medalist in gymnastics, was besieged by phone calls from advertisers and promoters when she entered the U. S. But they stopped calling when she openly admitted to having an affair with a married Florida man who had four children. Her perfect image as one of the world's greatest achievers and mentors was badly tarnished.

For years, the image of Steve Garvey gave him an income advantage. However, once the media learned of Steve's personal life, his once positive image was severely damaged. His wife, Cindy, who had revealed his affairs to an unbelieving press was vindicated and Steve lost that never to be regained all important money-making Mr. Clean reputation, at least for now.

Professional athletes with a positive image and reputation can easily add millions of dollars to their annual incomes, but in the past decade it became difficult for advertisers to find young athletes they could believe in and trust, so they turned to coaches and aging sports heroes.

Image certainly worked for Oliver North. He is a speaker's bureau's dream: well-groomed, good looking, articulate, believable that all-encompassing Boy Scout image. Four speeches a month at $25,000 each is pretty good retirement pay.

Twenty years ago nobody would have believed that Tommy Lasorda would be making $15,000 to give a speech for Fortune

500 companies and that his face would be gracing a weight-reduction commercial on television. I am sure he would never have believed it himself. A celebrity with a respected lifestyle can achieve great wealth.

Do your long-term goals include being a superstar in business, athletics, or the arts? When considering your future, consider your present lifestyle. Will it help or hinder? Will it add or subtract? Could you be sacrificing long-term personal image for short-term gain? Monitoring your lifestyle image is good common sense. Little did Jimmy the Greek realize what one thoughtless sentence would do to his television career and reputation. The more you have to gain, the more you have to lose.

THE LIKABILITY FACTOR

Some of you have all the elements of a powerful, positive personal image in place, yet it just does not seem to be working. That can be really frustrating. What you may be missing is the most important aspect of personal success, the importance of being likable.

Do you have a pleasing personality? If asked what makes a successful executive, some would say education; others would mention business knowledge or background. Some people are convinced it is who you know. Maybe it is a combination of all four of these, but the most important single factor is a likable personality. Your personality has everything to do with your success.

Year after year, new success theories come along encouraging us to follow this path or that formula, and for those with likeable personalities, they often work. But for people who do not know the missing ingredient, there is failure time and time again.

Personality, by definition, is "the personal traits that make one socially appealing." There are at least four personality types, and there are many tests and books available to tell you which one you are, but your personality type is not the issue here.

What is the issue is the ability to recognize the positive people skills you have and develop them to their fullest. But do not overdo it and try too hard; part of being likable is being natural.

Likable people:
- smile easily and often
- have a good sense of humor
- are themselves, without pretense
- are fun
- compliment easily and often
- know common sense etiquette and how to use it
- are self-confident
- engage you in conversation about yourself quickly
- know their limitations and that they do not have all the answers
- laugh at themselves, and
- are approachable or touchable

To find yourself in the running for advancement, people do not have to love or adore you, but they must be fond of you. Bennett Cerf, longtime chairman of Random House, was not especially good looking or charismatic, but he was one of the nation's most sought after dinner guests. Why? Because of his most likable characteristic—his sincere interest in others. Former President Ronald Reagan was the most popular president upon leaving office in the history of the United States thus far. What was his most outstanding personal quality? He was likable.

There is a point in the image game where the Christian Dior suits and Gucci shoes are no longer effective, a point where personality must take over. It is amazing what some people are willing to overlook when they like you. When the time comes to select the next manager, chief executive offer, or job applicant, all things being equal, likability just might be the deciding factor.

Most people do not lose jobs due to incompetence; personality conflicts are generally the reason. Recently I was contacted by a woman with six years of experience working with speakers. Her credentials were outstanding, and I thought I might have some referrals for her. I called her present employer before I recommended her to friends. After hearing many positive comments from the employer, I finally asked the question, "If you were looking to fill the position for your own personal business, would you hire her?" After moments of hesitation, the manager said, "No."I asked why. The response was, "She has a hard time getting along with co-workers."

The most important quality of a leader is his or her people skills. As you consider your career and personal goals, take stock of your likability factor. Are you a likable person? If not, you can learn to be. Just a short word of caution: the world knows when something is genuine and when it is fake.

9

Image from the Inside Out

The mental picture you have of yourself is defined as self image and self image determines the confidence with which you lead, the enthusiasm with which you approach your job, and, indeed, the extent to which people like you and enjoy doing business with you. Without a doubt the most powerful imagizing comes from the inside out. This image is based on how you see yourself physically, and how highly you esteem yourself.

Nothing is as important to your success in life as believing in yourself. And nothing is as destructive as holding on to a negative, critical picture of yourself. If you see yourself as attractive, you will radiate that image to others, and that is how they will perceive you. It is equally important to hurdle the inevitable failures in life without developing a negative inner picture of your abilities. The greatest asset on your path to success is your confidence. And your confidence is dependent on the inner picture you have of yourself in two areas: your physical appearance and your ability to be a success.

COMFORT ZONES AND PERSONAL IMAGE

In my twenty-five years in the image business, I have seen many examples of inside out imagizing, but I have never seen a more dramatic example than Mary. The day Mary walked into my office I knew I had found my walking advertisement. I was twenty-five years old and the owner/director of a southern

California self-improvement school that specialized in crafting new external images through weight reduction, clothing coordination, and grooming instruction. Freud may have said "Anatomy is destiny," but we refused to accept that as nature's final answer!

I had been looking for some time for a dramatic success story for my new business—the kind of "before and after" photo spreads you see gracing the pages of National Enquirer. I was sure I had found it in Mary. At least fifty pounds overweight, with clothes and hairdo that could only be categorized as "middle-aged frump," Mary looked at least ten years older than her actual age.

With visions of a growing business dancing in my head, I immediately took Mary under my wing as my special project. She dieted, groomed, and invested in a new wardrobe, and within three months Mary had exceeded my wildest dreams. She was svelte, youthful, and chic; it was hard for me to believe she was the same woman. Mary's husband called, raving about the changes. All Mary's friends lavished praise on her. I had my success story and a smug inner feeling that I had probably changed the entire course of another human being's life.

The next few months my business boomed, and I lost touch with my star graduate. One drizzly winter day about six months later I was standing in the foyer of a downtown building waiting for a meeting to begin when in walked a woman who looked vaguely familiar. As recognition dawned, my mouth fell open. Before me stood Mary, her weight, dowdy clothes, make-up, and mousy hair absolutely identical to the woman who had walked into my office nine months earlier. "Mary!" I gasped. "What happened?"

I listened in shocked disbelief as her story poured out. Throughout her life, Mary had never imagined herself as an attractive woman, someone who could receive compliments from the opposite sex. When I changed Mary's appearance she began to receive so much positive attention, she grew increasingly uncomfortable. She eventually came to hate her new look and began to say to herself, "I'm not attractive. This is not the real me. This is only a game. None of these people understand. I'm going to go back and show them who I really am!"

During the months since graduating, Mary had deliberately bulked back up and frumped back out until her outer image matched the inner image she had nurtured all her life.

I learned a very important and very humbling lesson that day. I had transformed Mary's body, but I had not transformed Mary's image of her body. I had changed the outside without changing the inside. Although fabulously successful in creating a new look, I had taken Mary outside her "body comfort zone" the image of herself she was comfortable with.

That early failure in human engineering changed forever my approach to personal image-making. I now firmly believe, and have seen proven countless times in the past twenty years, that no matter how much pushing, pulling, and rearranging you do, the fundamental dynamic of personal image-making is mind over mirror.

This was demonstrated again when a business acquaintance confided over dinner, "I've just lost fifty pounds!"

"Congratulations!" I said. "Which diet plan did you use?"

"That's just it," he beamed. "I didn't use any. In fact, I didn't consciously change my eating habits or my exercise plan. The only thing I changed was my image of myself. I simply stopped seeing myself as a fat man and started visualizing myself as a thin, attractive man, desirable to women."

The Beauty Bias

Imprisoned in each of our subconscious minds are pictures of our mental and physical assets. We compare our pictures of ourselves with our ideal image, and the result is high or low self-esteem. This inner comparison can be especially devastating in a culture where Youth and Beauty reign as the twin goddesses of our national religion of success.

Where do you get the images you use for comparison? They come from advertising, television, and the movies all of which are dependent on the world of make-believe. The perfect body, skin, or age is only a figment of Madison Avenue's imagination.

The beauty bias is taught early in our society. Who are the heroes in Cinderella? The beautiful heroine, of course, and the handsome prince. The stepmother and stepsisters, on the other hand, are mean and ugly. What about Snow White? She is beautiful, kind, and loved by everyone, the witch has a huge nose with a wart and is hated by everyone. The list of misfits goes on and on: The Ugly Duckling, Dumbo (remember the ears?), and Rudolph the You-Know-What, all rejected by their peers for being less than attractive, while the gorgeous characters walk off with fame, wealth, popularity, and the best-looking mates.

Several years ago, two researchers published a fascinating study in *Psychology Today*. Ellen Berscheid and Elaine Walster studied the effect of the beauty bias in the classrooms of public schools. Their disturbing conclusions:

(1) Better grades are given to the better-looking students.
(2) When disturbances occur, teachers are more likely to assume the ugly children are responsible.
(3) Stricter punishment is given out to the less attractive pupils than to the more attractive, for the same offense.

This bias follows you in adulthood right into corporate America. A study by the University of Minnesota concluded that physically attractive people are viewed to be "significantly more sensitive, kind, interesting, strong, poised, modest, socially and sexually warm" than those viewed as unattractive. As a result, job recommendations by experienced personnel consultants have been found to be strongly influenced by a candidate's physical appearance, even when physical appearance has no relationship to job performance. The unwritten rules in corporate America are ruthless. Seldom will a person standing five feet six inches tall and weighing three hundred pounds make it to the executive suite, no matter how intelligent he or she may be.

Liposuction and plastic surgery for both women and men are at an all-time high. Need you ask why? It evidently pays off in many cases. One study found that at least half the working women who get facelifts can expect to receive salary increases in the immediate months following.

It is not just women who are discriminated against. Less attractive salespeople are almost always less successful than their handsome competitors. What is the result of all this? Few of us have escaped without developing some sense of inferiority about our physical attributes. Some of us imagine the psychologist leaning across his desk and saying gravely, "I'm sorry, Mr. Jones, but your tests show that you don't have an inferiority complex. You're just plain inferior."

That negative inner picture of ourselves is our own worst enemy. It results in the Marys of our world never being able to break out of the old mold and build a positive, successful, confident new image.

STEPS TO A NEW PERSONAL IMAGE

There are two crucial steps in building a new physical image. First, you need to do something about the physical attributes you can change. You are not responsible for your height, skin color, or body frame, so you need to stop wasting your time thinking negatively about those attributes.

However, you are responsible for your body's upkeep. You may need to lose some weight; there are hundreds of plans and companies available to help you achieve this goal. You may even want to take advantage of the advances in plastic surgery to get rid of your baggy eyelids or saggy jowls or receding hairline. Maybe it is not possible to justify these steps on the basis of health alone. But if a relatively minor operation could add significantly to your self-confidence, why not take advantage of it? Positive feelings about your physical self are incredibly important to your future success.

Arthur Mitchell, the first black man to be accepted into the New York City Ballet, was interviewed on television regarding his now-famous Dance Theatre of Harlem. The interviewer asked how he had taken young people off the streets of Harlem and turned them into successful stars. I will never forget his reply, which focused on the necessity of having a positive physical image: "I have found if I can teach these kids to fall in love with their miraculous bodies, they will not fill them up with drugs."

This leads you to your second step in transforming your physical image. Once you have changed what you are able to change about your body, you must make a conscious decision to love and accept the physical self you have. I am not talking about preening and narcissism. I am talking about getting off the comparison and self-hate merry-go-round and really liking who you are physically.

With all this emphasis on the superficial, what happens to those of us who look in the mirror and conclude we were not born equal, we were not blessed with physical perfection? What if a hand or a leg is missing? What about the exceptionally tall or short?

I have already mentioned I am six feet tall, but what I did not say was I was six feet tall at the age of thirteen, exceptionally thin, and had a mouthful of braces. Do you know the average height of a boy in junior high school? At one of my first dances, a boy suggested he stand on a chair while I held his hand and danced in a circle around him.

Positive Choices and Positive Messages

We all come to a point of acceptance or rejection of our bodies at some point in life. At thirteen I made a choice to see my height as a positive thing. I decided to think that with my height, I might be a model someday. It was a choice to accept my difference and enjoy what is offered. The only alternative would have been a life of self-hate. That is especially tragic when it comes to developing a positive personal image. How you see yourself dramatically affects how you look.

I will never forget a "Phil Donahue Show" I saw a few years ago. Phil's guest that day was a woman who had suffered from Multiple Personality Disorder. At one point psychologists were able to identify twenty-one distinct personalities within this one person. I was especially interested as the woman showed photographs of herself. In each personality, she looked entirely different; each photograph showed a unique person. She appeared to be twenty-one completely different people. As I reflected on the show I was struck again with the power of the brain to change the image we project.

The internal picture of yourself that you carry in your heart and mind does not just affect your peace of mind and your level of self-acceptance. That would be significant enough by itself. The picture you carry of yourself actually changes the way you look. If you feel attractive, you will radiate that feeling . . . and that indeed will be the image others have of you.

Change the things you are able to change. After that, reprogram the messages your brain sends your body. Without embarrassment, for the sake of a transformed physical image, begin telling yourself that you look great, that you are attractive, and that you really do like the body you have been given. I guarantee that, as you change the way you see yourself inside and project that new confidence to others, you will notice a significant difference in the way others treat you. The perception others have of you depends almost entirely on how you see yourself.

The greatest power in any business is people power: confident, self-motivated, enthusiastic, friendly people. Confidence, more than intelligence or an M.B.A., is your single greatest career asset. I often hear corporate executives complain that their employment candidates look perfect on paper: the right college, degree, age, and appearance. The applicant seems to have everything . . . except a healthy ego. The opportunities are absolutely unlimited for a person with inner confidence. That is the person corporations most want to hire, Harvard graduate or not. You do not have to have overwhelming intelligence or "inside connections" to achieve success.

Dr. Ralph Showers is a living inspiration. Afflicted with a severe learning disability, at age fourteen he was unable to put a square peg in a square hole, or a round peg in a round hole. He was considered hopelessly unteachable. He is still unable to read, write, or spell with any accuracy. In addition, due to a tragic accident as a young adult, Dr. Showers has no hands or arms. But when his teachers gave up, his parents took over. They poured on the love and encouragement and taught him to believe in himself despite his handicaps.

And in 1984, in front of a television audience of ten million people on the "This Is Your Life" television show, Ralph Showers received his doctorate. He went on to found Rainbow Acres, a farm for mentally neglected people, and he now directs businesses across the U. S. and Japan.

Self Esteem and the Failure Factor

Personal image is simply the way others perceive you, and the way others perceive you begins with how you perceive yourself. No one will ever value you one bit higher than you value yourself.

While at Disneyland I met a highly efficient administrator named Lynn. Thirty-two years old when I met her, Lynn was just leaving a destructive marriage. The inner picture she carried of herself, as seen in her physical appearance and overall demeanor, was just about as low as it could be.

Lynn's boss at Disneyland was a classic "lead by intimidation" executive who was not known for handing out large doses of praise and appreciation. Almost daily, Lynn would slink out of the office uttering things to herself like, "Why can't I ever do anything right?" and "What's wrong with me?" The failure factor had obviously overwhelmed her.

After a while I could not take it any longer. Lynn was sweet, kind, and competent, and she deserved to feel worthy, as we all do. So every day I began to find a reason to compliment Lynn. "That's a nice color on you . . . your hair looks wonderful today . . . you look as though you've lost weight." As I continued these small praises, I noticed her appearance begin to change. She began to see herself through positive eyes.

One day she came out of her boss's office after another bruising confrontation. She sank glumly into the chair beside my desk and once again mumbled "What's wrong with me, Bobbie?"

"Let's take a walk, Lynn," I said. As we trudged across the park, I looked at Lynn and said, "I have a new thought for you. You know, it may be that there's nothing wrong with you, Lynn. It may be that there's something wrong with your boss. If he were perfect, do you think he'd be treating you this way?"

Lynn didn't answer, but I could tell she was thinking, thinking hard, as if she had never thought of this possibility.

"Lynn, the next time he attacks, here is what I want you to do. I want you to say to yourself, 'I'm terrific. I wonder what's wrong with him?'" She promised to give it a try.

A couple of weeks later, the volcano blew again, and I watched closely as Lynn left her manager's office. I felt an inner thrill when I saw a glint of anger in her eye as she marched briskly by. I knew she was ready for the big step. I came out of my office, gripped her by both arms, looked her straight in the eyes and said, "Lynn, now what are you going to do about it?"

Her eyes locked on mine for several seconds, blazing with anger. Then she turned around, walked back into his office, and stood in front of his desk until he looked up from his papers.

"I do not appreciate the way you just treated me," she said firmly and evenly. "It is not nice, and I do not expect to be treated in that manner again." Then she turned and walked out, leaving her boss with a shocked look on his face.

The next week, Lynn's boss gave her a raise. She had gained his respect by valuing herself enough to stand up to him. You see, the problem was not entirely the boss's. It is truly difficult to respect people who do not respect themselves. When Lynn's inner picture of herself and her worth changed, so did her boss's. But Lynn had to be the one to do the changing.

How do you begin to change an inner negative picture that may have taken a lifetime to develop? It takes more than putting on a facade or perfecting an "everything's wonderful" sales pitch. You need to deal with the roots of your failure complex by looking at how your critical self-portrait began.

Many of you in responsible positions in the business world today were raised by demanding, perfectionistic parents. You have scenes embedded in your memories of your parents going

crazy when you brought home less than perfect report cards.
The focus was on what you had done wrong, not what you had
done right. The same was true for many of you in athletics, as
your parents pushed you to excel and criticized you for your
failures.

In addition to this "work harder/be better" emphasis, many
of you were raised with the "don't compliment yourself" motto.
If you did something wrong, it was fine to tell yourself "That
was stupid!" or "What a total jerk I am!" But if you did something right, you were not allowed to tell yourself, "Hey, that was
great!" The result is that now, as adults, seventy percent or more
of your self-talk is negative. And negative self-talk, of course,
reinforces that "I am not good enough" inner picture.

That kind of upbringing produced a generation of High
Achievers, but two distinctly different kinds of High Achievers:
the "Driven" and the "Drawn." Those of you who are Driven
High Achievers tend to be perfectionists. You have heard the
definition of a perfectionist: one who takes great pains and gives
them to others? Many of you fit this definition of compulsive
workaholics, driven by impossibly high standards for yourselves, always falling short. The other type of High Achiever is
not "driven," but "drawn," drawn by goals and dreams, but not
obsessed with them. There are two litmus tests to determine
which of these two kinds of High Achiever you might be. The
two tests involve how you respond to success and how you respond to failure.

Those of you who are Driven High Achievers respond to success with no inner feelings of enjoyment and no boost to your
self-esteem. No matter how great the success, it was not good
enough. You do not stop to savor your achievements; you immediately and compulsively push on toward the next goal.
Those of you who are Drawn High Achievers tend to more easily
enjoy your success and allow your achievements to increase
your positive sense of worth. You take the time to smell the
roses along the way to your success.

The response to failure is even more revealing. Driven High
Achievers often react to failure with rage and self-hate or depres-

sion, then make everyone around them miserable. Drawn High Achievers are certainly disappointed by failure, maybe even deeply disappointed, but their sense of worth is not wholly dependent on being perfect or on winning unanimous praise and approval from others. They learn from their failures and move on without engaging in destructive self-talk. These are generalizations, and no one fits any generalization one hundred percent of the time. But one or the other of these models fits many in corporate America today.

The Struggle of Self Love

The key question is, how do you break the destructive patterns and become less "Driven" and more "Drawn"? I had a breakthrough insight on this one day while in my "think tank." I have developed the habit of spending one hour every day just thinking. One of the only places I can do so uninterrupted is to get in the bathtub. One day I was sitting in the tub when it came to me. I jumped out of the tub, looked at myself in the mirror, and said, "Bobbie, you're wonderful. Bobbie, you're fabulous. You're a great wife, a great mother, a great speaker, and a great boss. In fact, Bobbie, you are kind, generous, organized, and a born leader!"

I had discovered the meaning of the words: "As a man thinketh in his heart, so is he." I realized that the only way I would ever break my negative inner programming and become a total success as a wife, mother, boss, and speaker was to tell myself those things. I had heard the advice before. My problem was, I was not following it.

What this biblical advice suggests is that in order to feel wonderful, kind, generous, and so on, you must truly believe in your heart and mind that you are those things. Your brain tells you how to think about yourself. How you think about yourself radiates to those around you.

If you do not feel you are terrific, great, wonderful, and talented, how can you possibly make others feel that way about you? This is not conceit or narcissism. This is simply building a healthy ego by being proud of your accomplishments.

Every day you are responsible for programming your mental computer. If you choose negative, negative will return to you. You certainly can convince yourself that you are not wonderful or terrific or attractive or talented. It is easy to believe the negative. But what can you possibly achieve with that attitude? There is no denying the fact that talking about your failures in life seems more acceptable than praising your successes. The danger is that some people actually develop a sense of pleasure from failure. They become so negative they are allergic to themselves. Like the Driven High Achievers, they can never find anything nice to say about themselves. Consequently, neither can anyone else.

After climbing back into my think tank, I tried to figure out how to overcome this "failure factor". How do we prevent our failures in life from destroying our inner sense of worth? I began to think about the "Love Chapter" in the Bible, I Corinthians, chapter 13. It suddenly struck me that, although these verses are usually applied to how to love others, they are equally practical instructions on how to love oneself.

I went through the verses one at a time and applied each item to my own struggle to love and accept myself. The following is the result a "self-love" version of I Corinthians 13:

> Love is patient, so I will be patient with myself.
> Love is kind, so I will be kind to myself.
> Love is not envious, does not brag, and is not arrogant. I will not practice these traits, as they are self-destructive.
> Love is never haughty, selfish, or rude, so I will not talk rudely to myself or indulge in negative self-talk.
> When I love another, I am never to hold a grudge.
> And when I disappoint myself, I will release that grudge by forgiving myself.
> Love means remaining loyal, no matter what the cost.
> And because love always believes totally in the other person, always expects the best, and endures others' shortcomings.

I will also believe in myself, expect the best of myself, and bear with my own shortcomings.

How do you break the destructive cycle of inner blame and build a healthy inner picture of yourself and your abilities? Forgive yourself for your failures and give yourself the freedom to be less than perfect. As Colette Dowling says in *Perfect Women* (though it could have been titled Perfect Men as well):

"There's something spectacularly freeing about acknowledging that one has both resources and limitations, and that both of these give shape to one's life."

If you stop trying to live up to someone else's standard, or to an unrealistic standard you impose on yourself, you are freed to love and value yourself and to radiate that confident personal image to those around you.

10

The Balancing Game

I had just finished a presentation on image to the board of a major U.S. corporation when the CEO asked if we could talk privately. As soon as the two of us settled into his office, this highly successful executive leaned forward with a look of pain on his face and said, "Bobbie, I've played the image game right to the top. I've worked hard for twenty-five years to get to this point. I drive an image car, wear the right suits, and live in the right section of town. But what does any of it mean? Somewhere along the line I lost my wife and children. We're complete strangers."

Because of many, many conversations like this with successful business men and women in recent years, I must end this book with a note of warning. While image-making can be a powerful servant on the path to success, like any tool it is subject to abuse.

PLAYING THE GAME FOR THE WRONG REASONS

I am as serious in my conviction that it is smart to play the image game for business reasons as I am that you must also be very careful of the fundamental reasons why you are involved in the game. In your quest for success, it is very easy to forget what is truly important.

Playing for the wrong reasons can disrupt and even destroy personal relationships. If you are using image as a way to enhance personal esteem, it will not work. If you are using your abilities to purchase status items to impress, it will not work for the long term. What is real and what is imitation will always reveal itself in time.

After speaking to a group of wives of physicians in Texas, a woman came to me to ask if I would please change my plans to return to California and go to Amarillo instead. She wanted me to talk with her twenty-six-year-old stepson. She truly feared he was a candidate for suicide. She confided to me that her husband and stepson were totally unable to communicate or relate. She seemed desperate that I change my schedule. I flew to Amarillo; she stayed at the convention.

I was greeted at the airport by the doctor/husband, escorted to his expensive automobile, and driven to a lovely, large home in an elite area of town. The doctor explained that his son was unable to hold a job, had left school, and was generally wasting his life. The doctor seemed intelligent, pleasant, and he sincerely had my sympathy. I was totally unprepared for the long-haired, unclean, and totally lifeless twenty-six-year-old man I met the next morning. He was very thin, and his eyes were almost colorless.

My task was to spend the day with him to see if I could motivate him in any way. Being in public with this man was not easy for me. Ignoring his appearance, I asked him where he would like to go. He chose the museum and as we walked and talked, he told me of his interest in costumes and of his general likes and dislikes.

As I accepted this man just as he was, I noticed the strangest thing happening. His eyes began to take on color. At noon, I took him to a very nice restaurant. Although he was not appropriately dressed, he needed to be shown that he was accepted unconditionally. By the time lunch was over, he had agreed to cut his hair and purchase new clothes.

As he opened up to me, I began to understand his total lack of self-respect, self- confidence, and self-esteem. His father had become a doctor for all the wrong reasons, primarily to impress others. He constantly pushed the "proper people," the "right schools," the social status events, and "acceptable" friends down the throats of his five children. They did little to please him.

By the time we returned to the house, the doctor's son's eyes were clear and bright blue. His appearance was completely changed with the new clothes and haircut. The son was feeling pretty good about himself.

The doctor arrived home and, with all of the positive comments he could have made when he saw his son, his first remark was to suggest that the son button down his shirt collar. In a split second, I watched the young man's eyes return to a colorless grey and his body stiffen to a rod.

In my investigation of this family, it became clear that this poor doctor was so full of low self-esteem that no amount of status or wealth could conceal the facade of success or fill his personal void. The projection of success will never fill a self-esteem void; self-love must be unconditional.

Play the image game for business success, play it because you deserve it, or play it for pure pleasure. But playing because of insecurity, inferiority, or the need to impress are the wrong reasons. An image facade will never fill an empty soul.

Dr. Janice Halper studied 4,126 Fortune 500 male executives and published her results under the title *Quiet Desperation: The Truth About Successful Men*. The study revealed the following:

> Forty-eight percent of all middle managers said that despite years spent striving to achieve their professional goals, their lives seemed "empty and meaningless." Sixty-eight percent of senior executives said that they had neglected their family lives to pursue professional goals, and half said they would spend less time working and more time with their wives and children if they had it to do over again.

Because so many successful business people are experiencing dissatisfaction in these areas, it is absolutely essential that you consider some guidelines on how to protect your personal life in the midst of your business career.

There is no doubt that playing the image game can help you achieve success. In fact, attention to image is absolutely essential in today's business world. But you need to be careful, lest, when you get to the top of your ladder, you find it has been leaning against the wrong wall.

One businessman who had made it to the top of his field expressed it to me this way: "Bobbie, what I thought I wanted, what I thought was important, never turned out to be what I wanted at all once I got it. Then I'd go looking for something else to fill my void something, anything, that would give me that feeling of success. And it just went on and on. I joined private clubs and civic clubs and became well known. I showed up at social events with the most beautiful women in town. I gave my time to charity and made sure my picture appeared in the papers. But none of it ever seemed to give the satisfaction that I thought would come with success. Thank God I woke up before the ulcers and stress of success got me. I finally realized that what I'd been searching for was around me all the time. It was inside me and inside those I cared for."

What I am talking about is the need for each of us to define success in our own terms. It is obvious that society defines success almost exclusively in terms of the acquisition of money. We find our heroes and role models inside the episodes of "Lifestyles of the Rich and Famous" and within the pages of Vanity Fair. There is nothing wrong with enjoying the fruits of success, but some have bought society's definition in such an all-consuming way that money becomes more than something to be enjoyed. It becomes an addiction. One writer in Fortune analyzed it this way:

> Like an addiction, [money] requires higher and higher doses for the same thrill. Psychoanalysts find that many money addicts are children of parents too preoccupied, overworked, or withdrawn to respond with the appropriate oohs and ahs to baby's smiles and antics . . . But, says

Dr. Arnold Goldberg, a Chicago psychoanalyst, "The ante always goes up because the need is never satisfied. The kid wants a human response; money is a non-human response."

Having been raised in the affluent environment of southern California and having had the experience of business success in my early twenties, I had adopted a strong materialistic desire for things. I had a conversation with another woman that caused me to rethink the path I was taking. She asked me to close my eyes and visualize myself at age eighty-five. "Now," she said, "visualize who is around you." I did not want to think about it, but I had to admit that at the rate I was going, I would be lucky to have anyone around me.

In the weeks following, the words and scenes from that experience echoed in my mind. I knew at age eighty-five all my possessions and acquired wealth would mean very little. My deepest desire would be to have love, love not based on obligation, but authentic love. I realized there was only one way I could guarantee those kinds of love relationships would be around me at age eighty-five: if I earned those relationships by making my children and my husband a higher priority in my life right then.

Do you know what billionaire H. L. Hunt said when asked how a man achieves success? First, he said, decide what you want. Second, determine what you are willing to give up to get it. Third, set your mind to it. And fourth, get going. It all sounded so simple. However, I realized the key was number two determining what I was willing to give up to get success.

I saw in a clearer way than ever before that I was unwilling to give up my family, my close relationships. Money could not buy those relationships at age eighty-five. I knew from business that what goes around, comes around: what you give, you get. If I wanted to have love around me later in life, I would need to begin giving it in the present. In short, I came to realize that success meant a balance between professional and financial achievements and family.

THE PRINCIPLES OF BALANCE

In the years since that pivotal conversation, I have found it is possible to play the image game successfully and also maintain a healthy personal life. But it is a difficult balancing act, and I have found three key principles to be valuable guidelines while walking this tightrope.

Principle #1: Preserve your own identity. A number of years ago I received a long distance call from a man in New York City. He had attended one of my seminars on business image and was calling to share his own experience. At an early age this man had an exceptional musical ability. Envisioning a career as a great concert pianist, his parents started him on a highly disciplined schedule of practices and recitals. With his parents as his promoters, this young man played the image game in the music world for twenty years.

Now firmly in midlife and very frustrated, this individual finally realized he had pursued a career and an image forced on him by his parents. Although it took a large amount of courage, he was now making a career shift at age forty. He realized that what he did in life needed to flow out of his own identity and not his parents' desires for him.

One very real danger in playing the image game is that you can lose your identity. As you saw in the last chapter, Driven High Achievers are especially vulnerable in this area. They are proficient at fulfilling others' expectations and never giving themselves the freedom to discover and follow their own unique dreams.

It is important that you not turn your imagizing efforts into an "Adopt-An-Image" game that promotes a totally false identity for yourself. The image you project does involve putting your best foot forward. But it should be your best foot, not someone else's. Know who you are; pick a career you can honestly enjoy; then build your Image Master Plan around those solid realities.

Principle #2: Keep life in balance. Psychology Today conducted an in-depth survey of 1,139 top executives across the country.

These individuals were all CEOs and earned salaries between $141,261 and $356,029. Psychology Today asked these highly successful business people their primary advice to others still climbing the corporate ladder. The response of the overwhelming majority: learn to balance your life and your lifestyle. If you want to last for the long haul in your career, take care of your body, mind, and soul—the mental, physical, and spiritual parts of your life.

Executives with the most energy and staying power have learned to take care of themselves in a balanced way. Burnout has marred the careers of many promising business people on the way to the top. Taking time to feed your mind, to keep your body in shape, and to cultivate your relationship with God will provide a measure of strength that may make the difference between flaming out or holding out in the image game.

Principle #3: Make room for relationships. Whatever your definition of success, you will never be happy without one or more close relationships in your life. In fact, the principles involved in successfully playing the image game in business can help you immensely in building successful personal relationships as well.

The Keys to Love

Successful business and personal relationships both require learning to discern the emotional needs of those you are close to and seeking to meet them. The needs of your employees, the need for praise and appreciation, for respect, for communication are exactly the same needs your loved ones feel the most strongly. Finding and meeting those needs create the glue that builds strong, unbreakable bonds with those you are closest to. It is just a matter of putting some shoe leather on your love and learning to express in concrete ways what you feel inside.

There are a couple of secrets in expressing love that work wonders even for damaged relationships or deadlocked marriages. First, say it verbally. You need to "break the sound barrier" in communicating love to those closest to you. Talking to your loved ones and listening to them is perhaps the most prized gift you can offer. Relationships flourish as you give them attention, and they die as they are neglected. The same is true in your relationship with your children.

The National Parent-Teachers Association conducted a survey a few years ago in which it was determined that American parents spend an average of seven and one-half minutes per week communicating with each of their children. If that sounds unbelievable, perhaps you need to think back on your past week. How much time did you spend talking with your children, eyeball to eyeball, just to find out how each was doing?

It helps to remember that what goes around, comes around. If you want to have loved ones around when you are old, you need to be giving that love now. And giving it verbally is one of the best ways.

I was taking a break after speaking in Dallas a few years ago when a beautiful young woman with extremely short hair came into the lounge where I was resting. I commented on how attractive she looked, adding that not many women can wear their hair that short and still look so good.

"Are you kidding?" she asked.

"Not at all," I replied. "You really look great."

She was quiet for a moment, as if considering whether to talk to me or not. Then she said she had been in my seminar that morning, and she wondered if we could talk for a few minutes. When I agreed, she plopped down in the chair next to mine and proceeded to pour out the most amazing story.

"My hair is short because it's just growing back after having been shaved for my brain surgery," she said. "I'm also in recovery from anorexia. The doctors think the brain tumor was partially caused by my anorexia." Tears welled up in her eyes. "It was a pretty bad case," she said. "I almost died."

She went on to explain that when she came home from her high school graduation at age eighteen, she found her bags packed and waiting on the front porch. A note from her father said simply: "You're responsible for taking care of yourself from now on."

She told me how deeply this had hurt her, and that she had

made up her mind to reach this insensitive, unfeeling man in some way. Her first attention-getting stunt was to get herself arrested for shoplifting. When that did not produce the effect she wanted, she stopped eating. Totally. Eventually she had to be hospitalized.

"I was lying in my hospital bed near death with all kinds of tubes coming out of my body when my father finally came to see me. We talked for about an hour. Then he got up to leave. As he opened the door to my room, I guess I just went berserk. 'You just can't say it, can you?' I screamed. 'I'm going to die and you still can't say it!'

" 'Say what?' he asked, stunned.

" 'You can't say 'I love you!' You never have and I guess you never will.' "

I asked her if he ever did tell her he loved her.

"Oh yes. If he hadn't, I wouldn't be alive today. He came back to my hospital bed and began to cry like a baby when he realized that I had almost died, that I was willing to risk my life, just to hear my dad tell me he loved me. At that very moment I began to recover from my anorexia, but I had already begun to form a brain tumor."

I kept in touch with this young woman, and she appeared to have recovered completely. But there are thousands of other young people today who do succeed in destroying themselves. Many of them could have been saved simply by hearing the magical words "I love you."

The second key to expressing love is to say it with touching and affection. The sense of touch is as important to your well-being as is your sight, hearing, taste, and smell. Yet touch is the most neglected and abused of all of your senses. Babies die when they are not touched. Elderly people confide that one of the worst parts of growing old is having no one around to touch them, to show them physical affection.

I have made a hobby of watching families in airports saying hello and goodbye. When it comes time for the customary hugs, there are always families that obviously find it very awkward to touch. It just has not been a part of their family experience. I firmly believe there are emotional needs that are going unmet because of the absence of touching in those families.

In analyzing my own childhood, I realized that, although I knew my parents loved me, they never said the words and seldom hugged me. I made a vow not to make that mistake with my own children. Every day they get their hug and a verbal "I love you." Then I set out to change my relationship with my parents. It took a fair amount of courage to end a phone conversation with the first "I love you," but once I did there was an amazing change. The next step was the full- blown bear hug, not just the polite peck on the cheek. Someone has to start. Someone has to care enough to be the first.

When I was in my twenties I decided to take a week off from my job and volunteer as a counselor at a summer camp for high school girls. A large seventeen-year-old girl especially caught my eye. All week long this girl wore a sweatshirt that read "I Need A Hug." One day we were walking together back to the mess hall. The young girl said something I thought was funny, and I spontaneously put my arm around her back and gave her a little squeeze. Suddenly, I found this seventeen-year-old in my arms crying. Panicking, my first thought was, "Way to go, Your first experience as a counselor, and you've obviously blown it royally!"

When the girl finally calmed down, I asked her what was wrong.

"My mother never touches me," she sniffled. "From the time I was old enough to dress myself, my mother never again touched me with love."

This poor girl was so in need of having arms wrapped around her that she turned to a total stranger to fill her need. Teens have told me that they were so in need of a hug they turned to the only place they knew to get it, to the opposite sex. Then, not knowing how to handle it, they found themselves in trouble.

I was deeply touched as I read the following letter from a man in Ann Landers's column:

Dear Ann Landers:

A few weeks ago I kissed my son for the very first time and told him I loved him. Unfortunately, he did not know it because he was dead. He had shot himself. The greatest regret of my life is that I kept my son at arms' length. I believed it was unmanly for males to show affection for one another. I treated my son the way my father treated me, and I realize now what a terrible mistake it was. Please tell your male readers who were raised by "macho" dads that it is cruel to withhold affection from their sons. I will never recover from my ignorance and stupidity.

No name, no city, no state

I have had hundreds of people tell me they never heard the words "I love you" from either of their parents. They tell me that because they were fed and clothed and housed, they were supposed to assume that love was automatic and went with the credit card. But as Dr. Goldberg said earlier, "The kid wants a human response; money is a non-human response."

As a young man, Al was a skilled artist, a potter. He had a wife and two fine sons. One night, his oldest son developed a severe stomachache. Thinking it was only some common intestinal disorder, neither Al nor his wife took the condition very seriously. But the malady was actually acute appendicitis, and the boy died suddenly a short time later that night.

Knowing the death could have been prevented if he had only realized the seriousness of the situation, Al's emotional health deteriorated under the enormous burden of his guilt. On top of all that, Al's wife ran off with another man a short time later, leaving him alone with his six-year-old son. The hurt and pain of the two situations were more than Al could handle, and he turned to alcohol to help him cope. In time, he became an alcoholic.

As the alcoholism progressed, Al began to lose everything he possessed—his home, his land, his art objects everything. Eventually, Al died alone in a San Francisco motel room.

When I heard of Al's death, I reacted with the same disdain the world shows for one who ends his life with nothing material to show for it. "What a complete failure!" I thought. "What a totally wasted life!"

As time went by, I began to reevaluate my earlier harsh judgment. You see, I knew Al's now adult son, Ernie. He is one of the kindest, most caring, most loving men I have ever known. I watched Ernie with his children and saw the free flow of love between them. I knew kindness and caring had to come from somewhere.

I had never heard Ernie talk much about his father. It is so hard to defend an alcoholic. One day I worked up my courage to ask him. "I'm really puzzled by something," I said. "I know your father was basically the only one to raise you. What on earth did he do that you became such a special person?"

Ernie sat quietly for a few moments, reflecting, then said, "From my earliest memories as a child until I left home at eighteen, Al came into my room every night, gave me a kiss, and said, "I love you, son."

Tears came to my eyes as I realized what a fool I had been to judge Al as a failure. He had not left any material possessions behind. But he had been a kind, loving father, and he left behind one of the finest, most giving men I have ever known. I know this story because I married Al's son. For over thirty years I have benefitted from the love Al modeled to Ernie.

As far as I am concerned, success is a goal worth aiming for in life. How do I define success? Success is the realization, or attainment, of any worthy goal. For me, that includes enjoying the fruits of material success. In today's business world, playing the image game is absolutely essential to attaining that material success.

I also know that I never want to play the game in such a way that I lose the other things that make life worth living. I know that the greatest rewards of my life will be the rewards of coming home to a house filled with love, peace, and joy. When I die, no matter what my financial statement looks like, I know I will have been successful if my personal life was filled with gentleness, kindness, goodness, dependability, and most of all, love unconditional, nonjudgmental, authentic love. Now that is what I call success.

Bobbie Gee makes keynote presentations, conducts Winning the Image Game seminars, and does image consulting with large and small organizations world wide. For more information on products and services offered by Bobbie Gee Enterprises please contact:

Bobbie Gee Enterprises
1540 South Coast Highway
Suite 206
Laguna Beach, California 92651

(714) 497-1915
FAX (714) 497-9155
(800) 462-4386